PARENTING CHALLENGING CHILDREN WITH POWER, LOVE AND SOUND MIND:

THE NURTURED HEART APPROACH™ FROM A BIBLICAL VIEWPOINT

Wendy A. West Pidkaminy, LCSW

Kristine M. Smith, Editor-in-Chief

Nurturing Life Designs, LLC
New York

Parenting Challenging Children with Power, Love and Sound Mind:
The Nurtured Heart Approach™ from a Biblical Viewpoint

Library of Congress Catalog Number: 2009909414

ISBN: 978-0-615-33314-4

REL012030   RELIGION / Christian Life / Family

Published by Nurturing Life Designs, LLC, Manlius, NY

Book and Cover Design by Butch Braun of Epoch Advertising: Syracuse, New York
www.epoch-adv.com

For information about bulk purchasing discounts of this book, orders within the book industry or other products from Nurturing Life Designs, LLC please contact Nurturing Life Designs at wendy@nurturinglifeconcepts.com, (315) 682-4005 or 131 West Seneca Street Suite 139 Manlius, New York 13104

The Nurtured Heart Approach™ and information in this book relating to the NHA are all used with the express permission of Howard Glasser, M.A

The Nurtured Heart Approach™ is a trademark of the Children's Success Foundation.

All scripture quotations, unless otherwise indicated, are taken from the
HOLY BIBLE, NEW INTERNATIONAL VERSION®. NIV®.
Copyright © 1973, 1978, 1984 by International Bible Society.
Used by permission of Zondervan. All rights reserved.

Scripture taken from the New King James Version.
Copyright © 1982 by Thomas Nelson, Inc.
Used by permission. All rights reserved.

Scripture Quotations marked (NLT) are taken from the Holy Bible,
New Living Translation, copyright © 1996.
Used by permission of Tyndale House Publishers, Inc.,
Wheaton, Illinois 60189. All rights reserved.

All names and certain circumstances have been changed to protect the identities of families in this book, except for professionals and Advanced Trainers of the NHA.

Testimonials

We have known Wendy for a number of years. First and foremost, she is a committed Christian who follows the principles of the Word. Wendy is dedicated and steadfast in her Christian walk and is an example to others as a wife and parent. We are so grateful to have the opportunity to interact with Wendy.

— **Carl and Jeanne Bargabos, Assistant Pastors at Abundant Life Christian Center.**

Wendy is a gifted teacher, facilitator and human being. I pray that *Parenting with Power, Love and Sound Mind* blesses and heals families galore!

— **Robert de Wetter, Parent/Head Pastor of Snow Mass Chapel, Colorado.**

The Nurtured Heart Approach™ is transforming children, families, and classrooms across the country. It fosters inner strength to ensure success in all aspects of life. Wendy West-Pidkaminy shifts the perspective of the people with whom she interacts and helps lead the charge on a Greatness Revolution. Through her determination, compassion, and creative energy, Wendy has framed the approach in a new way and is changing the communities around her. Wendy is a pioneer who is blazing a new trail that will ultimately lead to a greater purpose for those who follow it.

— **School Psychologist/Parent/Director of Non-profit dedicated to helping children and families**

We are eternally grateful for the Nurtured Heart Approach™ and to have learned from Wendy Pidkaminy. The approach is easy to learn, extremely effective, and leads to immediate improvements. Wendy has a passion for sharing the approach and is an excellent facilitator, able to effectively teach others. She is beyond wonderful to work with and lives to nurture others. Wendy and these amazing NHA techniques have changed our lives for the better, forever. In less than a week nagging, yelling, frustration and disappointment were replaced with encouragement, loving communication, tranquility and satisfaction. Our children blossomed with joy and happiness and we found peace and contentment in our hearts and home. Our relationships with our children and with others have improved beyond what we imagined possible. Thanks to the NHA and Wendy, we can now help our children lead the life of greatness that God intended for them!

— **Parent/Professional Software Developer**

I was attending a conference when I first heard Wendy and her colleague provide information about the Nurtured Heart Approach™. I was intrigued to learn more. It's an approach I had been seeking for years: simple and easy to incorporate. I decided to use it with my three sons. In the past, I had railed against their negative behaviors, giving my sons endless lectures about what they did wrong. I gave multiple warnings and made their lives miserable if they didn't change their behaviors. I often felt guilty afterward. I knew I needed to change the way I handled this parenting business. As I evolved with the Nurtured Heart Approach™, I celebrated the GREAT things that my kids did. Now I lecture them on their greatness. My oldest son recently told me that I don't have to point out the good choices he makes because he knows he's now making better choices. Now that I'm focusing on the great things they do, my sons' resistance to hearing from me is gone. My relationships with my children and with my wife are better as a result of using the approach. My kids follow through when I ask them to do something. The old-style threat of consequences made things even worse in my home and didn't change anything. It was the same old thing day after day. I would say things like, "Here we go again." That same old garbage kept hitting the fan. Through my own transformation, I began to teach the approach to other parents. I rallied a group of parents to attend one of Wendy's workshops with me so they could use it with their children, some of whom are labeled as having Severe Emotional Disturbance (SED). They too grew from the experience. When I'm visiting families, they catch me using the various NHA approaches and can describe the technique I'm applying, which is a true validation of its easy-to-understand application. I love it so much that I took Advanced Training so I can teach others. Having learned about so many different approaches and models of working with people, the Nurtured Heart Approach™ is by far the simplest one to learn, and it resonates with my desire to be a better father to my children and a better associate to the people I work with. It's an approach that warms the heart. We all want to be recognized for being great, not for the mistakes we make. Wendy has an amazing ability to interact with her clients and their children. Her demeanor is that of a saint. She's passionate about the Nurtured Heart Approach™ and is able to reach out in a soft and affirming fashion. I felt comfortable in approaching Wendy before a job interview, and without hesitation she was able to build up my inner strengths, focusing on my greatness. Her ability to look at a person and discern their intrinsic greatness helped me feel confident during the interview process.

— **Parent/Social Worker**

Wendy is dynamic, a vortex of energy, and a volcano of creativity. Her compassion, as well as her innate ability to share her knowledge and skills in a profound way, sets her apart from her peers. Wendy has richly enlightened and blessed my life with her highly motivated stance at serving those around her. Her approach is extremely positive, always probing and insightful. Wendy is a person of absolute integrity, good character and a great sense of humor. She is gifted, inspired, and brings the best out of those she works with. Her enthusiasm is contagious and this permeates everything she touches from her creative projects right down to people's lives. An excellent, charismatic communicator, with a deep love of the Lord, I am thankful to have Wendy in my life.

— **Social Worker**

Wendy and the approach have changed our lives. As a single parent, foster parent and active grandparent caring for six children I needed a miracle. Wendy provided it with her bubbly personality and high skill level. She helped me take back my house and turn around my rambunctious bunch.

— **Parent/Grandparent/Foster Parent**

Wendy taught me the Nurtured Heart Approach™ and helped me transform my classroom into a true learning environment. I am happy to come to work again!!

— **Parent/Teacher**

Table of Contents

Acknowledgments

Howard Glasser: Without your openness to receive and create the Nurtured Heart Approach™ and your willingness to share it with others, this book would not have come to life. You are a world changer who has transformed the lives of countless individuals simply by encouraging them to be who God created them to be. Your friendship is a blessing to me and my family.

Lisa Bravo: Lisa, thank you for planting the seed and daring me to dream this "big person" book into life. You are a bright shining star that always lives life to the fullest with zest and zeal.

Pastors John Carter, Lisa Carter and the entire staff of Abundant Life Christian Center in East Syracuse, New York: Thank you for leading by example and for teaching so many of us the Word of God and how to live accordingly. You are magnificent role models, teachers and people who hear from God and share generously with all of us.

Pastors Carl and Jeanne Bargabos of Abundant Life Christian Center in East Syracuse, New York: Words cannot express my gratitude for the two of you. Your wisdom has blessed Brian and me time and time again. I am so grateful to God to have the two of you as spiritual mentors in my life.

Glenn and Shirley Litz, my parents: Thank you for providing me with a house filled with love and laughter. Your consistent encouragement to live out my dreams, and the model you have provided for me, has allowed me to become the person I am today. I have basked in the glow of your support and encouragement every step of the way. I love you both.

Dale and Rhonda West: For your guidance, advice and unconditional love. (not to mention the endless editing and support during this amazing process of growth and stretching into new territory) in every area of my life, thank you. I am a better person because of you two.

Michael Gilbert, Katherine Teasdale Edwards, and Andy Palumbo: Thanks to my delightfully talented co-collaborators who are always ready to jump into the next adventure head first.

Kristine Smith, Theresa Curley and Shirley Litz: This book is a glorious gift that will bring healing to the multitudes, because of your endless support, advice and assistance!

Dedication

This book is dedicated to my family. To Brian, my husband, best friend, number one supporter, co-laborer in the Lord and soul mate: I love and respect you with all my heart. To my graciously-gifted, fantastically fabulous children, Savannah and Chandler. Each of you is amazing, wonder-filled and a true reflection of Jesus Christ.

I am privileged to share life's journey with all of you. The three of you are evidence that God has created miracles in my life.

Preface

A few years ago, I attended a seminar called "Transforming the Difficult Child: The Nurtured Heart Approach™" presented by its founder, Howard Glasser. I must confess my primary intention that day was to spend some time with a former colleague and, on a secondary level, to gain an understanding about working with challenging individuals.

At the time, I was no stranger to intense children. Having two of my own and having worked a number of years in child welfare and school systems, I had tried every "trick in the book" to reach success. And quite frankly, I believed I was relatively successful working in the field of challenging families. I had a solid reputation for being a good clinician and for producing positive results.

But what Howard Glasser said blew me away! His approach, with its easy-to-use techniques, is totally based in common sense but contrary to traditional methods. This was a revelation to me and I laughed at the absurdity that I hadn't figured it out myself!

I realized that I had naturally followed many of Glasser's strategies and that I worked from a solution-focused, strengths-oriented stance, but I hadn't done it to the degree necessary to instill a sense of "inner wealth," "inner strength," "greatness" and "godliness" in others. I would give positive, nodding attention to situations that were deemed successes, but then would reduce the power of my approval by giving the same amount of energy and acknowledgement to things were not going well. In banking parlance, my "deposits" of positive commentary into my children's emotional bank accounts were "cancelled out" — at times even "overdrawn" — by the negative course-correction remarks that I made.

Glasser's singular seminar changed my life! I am now an Advanced Trainer of the Nurtured Heart Approach™ and Glasser is my mentor in this area. I share both Christian and non-religious versions of the approach with practitioners, teachers, parents and other caregivers, teens and children. I regularly work, consult and present in a variety of settings: schools, colleges, universities, government agencies, seminars, retreats, trainings and private practice.

My family is a Nurtured Heart Christian Family, superintended with power, love and sound mind. My daughter and son, although delightfully intense, are thriving; my home is filled with the peace and joy of God.

I allow Glasser's more non-religious methods to permeate my family and professional worlds because, as a lifelong Christian, I feel confident that it works in tandem with all I have been taught about God in the Scriptures. Perhaps without knowing it, Glasser has created a curriculum and techniques of communication and discipline that are firmly based on the Word of God. I know the easy-to-use techniques and tools you uncover within these pages will yield amazing results with your family because God has used, and continues to use, Christians and non-Christians alike to fulfill His purposes on earth.

God placed a burning desire within me to share Glasser's approach with the Christian community. I have spoken to many Advanced Trainers, teachers, pastors, human services professionals and seminar participants. All have said this book will be embraced and valued by the Church.

I have worked with many Christian parents who came to me hurt and broken. Their children were running the house, suffering at school and flunking Social Skills 101. As a Christian, you can safely learn, adopt and apply *Parenting Challenging Children with Power, Love and Sound Mind: The Nurtured Heart Approach™ from a Biblical Viewpoint* in your home while feeling confident that you're following God's plan and allowing your children to be blessed with abundance.

This goes without saying, but I'll say it anyway: I'm not a perfect parent or clinician. I make mistakes and my children make mistakes. No one is, or expects, perfection. We are all doing the best we can and finding ways to enjoy the fleeting moments we have together as a family or in a clinical setting. I continue to seek wisdom, knowledge, discernment and understanding.

I'm humbled and privileged to share what I've learned while using *Parenting with Power, Love and Sound Mind* with scores of parents, children and teens. The methods of communication and interaction you discover herein will produce tremendous results when combined with persistent reliance on God, using the power you have through Jesus Christ, and yielding to the Holy Spirit. As you know, God must always be your primary source of wisdom. As Christian parents, we're obligated to teach our children how to apply the Bible in their own lives. As you search your heart in prayer and reflect upon the Scriptures, God will awaken you to His vision for your family.

It's my sincere prayer that this book will help transform your life and the lives of your children, teens and family into the miracle-filled precious gems that you and God know them to be.

Thank you for being brave enough to want to change, determined enough to see it through, and loving enough to apply the best of what God has to offer to every area of your life.

I wish you miracles, blessings, prosperity, peace and abundance in all that you do!

— Wendy

Foreword

I first became acquainted with Wendy Pidkaminy when we both worked as child protective caseworkers investigating and serving severely abused children and their families. We were often taken aback by the extremes to which some parents would go in "disciplining" their children out of anger and frustration for what they viewed as disobedient or otherwise unacceptable behavior.

As committed Christians, Wendy and I share Biblical views of children as a rewarding gift from God and of parenting as one of life's greatest stewardship responsibilities (Psalm 127:3; Proverbs 22:6). With other like-minded co-workers, we began a noontime prayer meeting to build each other up in our faith (Jude 20). Although we no longer work together, we have remained connected.

Wendy's book was born out of Scriptural parenting and counseling methods she developed based on Howard Glasser's Nurtured Heart Approach™ for "transforming difficult children." Her desire is to help Christian parents embrace God's call to raise their children, even difficult ones, not with fear and trepidation but with power, love, and a sound mind (2 Timothy 1:7).

Our Lord wants us all to become like children. As adults, we are not to be childish in our actions and attitudes (1 Corinthians 13:11). However, we must always be childlike in our faith to receive all that God has for us; He warns us not to look down on children but, rather, to value them (Matthew 18:3-10). And He tells us to bring children to Him without hindering them (Mark 10:13-14).

When asked to identify the greatest of all commandments, Jesus quoted the commands to love the Lord our God with all our heart, soul, mind, and strength and to love our neighbors as ourselves (Mark 12:30-31). If we as believers take these commandments seriously, we must diligently teach these truths of God's Word to our children (Deuteronomy 6:4-7). Of course, our talk is cheap if it is not backed up by our actions.

My wife and I have been in the ministry for over thirty years, twenty of which I also spent in education, while we raised two now adult children (one a counselor, the other a special education teacher). Prior to becoming a caseworker, I taught students of all ages in both public and private schools and assisted home-schooling families with educating their children. Many of these parents would have benefited from this book.

Having worked with Wendy was a particular pleasure and privilege I enjoyed for nearly a decade and a memory I will treasure forever. I trust that readers of her book will see the sparkle in her eyes, hear the sweetness in her voice, and sense the conviction in her heart. It is an honor for me to recommend this book for parents struggling to raise children or teens to fulfill God's plans and purposes in their lives (Jeremiah 29:11; Romans 8:28).

Rev. Thomas Burgess

Pastor of Hope Christian Fellowship
(Canastota, NY)

Supervisor for Onondaga County
Department of Social Services
(Syracuse, NY)

October 15, 2009

Savannah's Story

My daughter, Savannah, has graciously allowed me to begin this book with a story about her and how our entire family struggled to help her. Before I asked her permission, I waffled back and forth about including the story because I didn't want to put unnecessary pressure on her or put her into a spotlight that she might not enjoy standing in. But then I decided to ask her what she thought. You see, Savannah is wise and gentle, kind and loving — always willing to help others and do the right thing. Without hesitation, Savannah said she would be delighted to have her story told to the world, as she believes her tale will help other parents and kids in similar situations. So here we go!!

Even before Savannah was handed to us in the delivery room, I knew she was a high-spirited gift from God. Savannah moved around so much in my womb that whenever she quieted, I would panic. I would drink juice or ice-cold water to perk her up, simply because I was so accustomed to her frequent tossing and turning. Peace and quiet were definitely not baseline behaviors for the bundle I carried under my heart!

From the moment Savannah was born, she was active. It seemed almost as though Savannah skipped crawling and walking and segued straight to running. If I turned my back for a split second at the playground, Savannah, a toddler, would be on the "big kids" play set, swinging on bars that were double, if not triple, my height. Eventually I became accustomed to her divine gifts of great athleticism, speed, balance and flexibility, but it took a lot of getting used to and more than a few minor panic attacks!

As Savannah grew, her adventurous pace wore out just about everyone in her path. I'm convinced the Energizer Bunny would give out before Savannah! She excelled at home where she was free to be herself, and in pre-school and kindergarten because she had loving and delightful teachers who cherished her. But when she moved to first grade, she had a teacher who was new to the field. She told me there was something wrong with my abilities as a parent because of Savannah's lack of self-discipline. The teacher began calling my child a "monkey," moved her to the back of the class facing a wall, and consistently ridiculed her in front of her classmates. Savannah would come home crying her eyes out, saying she was different, she didn't fit in, her former close friends were not playing with her as they had before. The list went on.

It was heartbreaking to watch and maddening to receive no respect nor a workable solution from the teacher. Even worse, I was a practicing social worker who helped families and children as a professional. How could this be happening to me?

I felt defeated, worn out, and overwhelmed many times — but I never gave up. I was adamant about not putting Savannah on medication, which is increasingly prescribed as a "cure" for children's behavioral "maladies." My husband and I began a quest to help Savannah harness her intensity and impulsiveness in as many ways as we could. We tried changing her diet, giving her natural supplements, and letting her exercise and run around and in the house before school started. We read parenting books and programs from A to Z. Most worked for a while, but not well enough to create real change.

Savannah was descending to the depths emotionally because of the toll her school experience was taking on her; and I was getting worse myself, watching her struggle hopelessly against her own natural proclivities. I finally caved in, made an appointment with a well-known psychologist, and came out with an evaluation that said Savannah had symptoms of ADHD and should be medicated. It was against everything we believed in, but we were so desperate for peace that we placed Savannah on medication. While there was improvement, the stigma of Savannah "being a monkey" remained, expressed and unexpressed. Medication couldn't fix her lowered self-esteem. It couldn't fix my feeling like a complete failure as a parent. Most importantly, medication didn't teach us how to honor Savannah's intensity as a gift from God and to channel it in healthy ways. The drug simply masked her intrinsic energy level and crippled the irrepressible dynamo that God had created!

Savannah was on medication for two years. Her personal "portfolio" (the vision she carried of herself based on the evidence she saw and heard from parents, teachers, and others) showed her to be a person who "acted crazy" and couldn't sit still. She saw herself as a misunderstood "alien" who wasn't able, or worthy, to fit in.

Birthday parties galore came and went, but few classmates invited Savannah to join the festivities. Savannah handled it all well, but it was obvious that, deep down inside, she was in pain.

Then I went to Howard Glasser's seminar and learned the Nurtured Heart Approach™. I came home, excited to tell my family that Glasser was transforming children with ADHD and scores of other challenges just by communicating differently.

We took Savannah off the medication with her pediatrician's approval and began letting her know about the many things we saw that were going right in her life. We told her in great detail about all of the characteristics, talents, God-given gifts and abilities she possessed. And Savannah began to change: she began to sit still, relax and feel good about herself.

In the third grade, we moved Savannah to a different school. We didn't tell the new teacher about her previous history. Since then she has consistently received good grades and has started a new life. As I put the finishing touches on this book, Savannah is entering seventh grade. She has lots of friends, and an abiding love for God and for others. She is flourishing as a beautiful young lady — inside and out. And yes, she is still intense. She's high-spirited and adventurous — and that's exactly what God intended her to be! Savannah is blessed with intensity and she'll be able to do all she sets out to do because of her non-stop energy. Presently, she is in numerous sports and school activities, volunteers at church and local non-profit agencies, and works occasionally as a babysitter, mows lawns, does house cleaning and other odd jobs. The good news is that, because of the Nurtured Heart Approach™ her intensity is now properly channeled and she can change her world with it. There are now no symptoms of ADHD in Savannah's life and there have not been for years.

Nick's Story

Nick, an educated, dedicated, faith-filled Christian dad, with a son, 9, and a daughter, 15, has allowed me to share yet another familiar story:

"I hate always being 'the bad guy.' The guy who has to say 'No' or 'Stop' or 'You're too young,' more often than I can say 'Sure, go ahead. Have fun!' My kids are now at ages where they question my decisions at almost every turn. Both my son and daughter have friends influencing them who don't share the values I'm trying to instill. Some of my daughter's classmates are 'dating' on a serious level already; some are becoming pregnant, abusing drugs and alcohol, and engaging in a host of other dangerous behaviors! It scares me half to death to think that she may be more influenced by peer pressure and mainstream media than she is by me. She doesn't understand the male teenage mind or his hormones the way I do. How do I warn her about the hazards of the teenage years without scaring her away from her God-given drive to find a life partner who will honor, cherish, and respect her? My inclination is to terrify her into nun-like behavior for the next several years! But what I really want to do is to let her know, and learn to believe for herself, that she is a beautiful person, inside and out, filled with great qualities and strengths. She's worthy of a guy who will wait for her until marriage."

Nick's nine-year-old was also a source of concern. He had become compulsively addicted to computer games and the Internet. Getting him away from the computer and outside for physical activity became a terrible battle of wills, with tempers flaring on both sides.

Nick realized his problem and admitted to us, "The more I lecture, punish, and try to guide my children, the farther they pull away from me emotionally and engage more in behaviors that are damaging at best and dangerous at worst. Quite frankly, the kids seem deaf when I talk to them, even when I come across like a no-nonsense military commander. What's worse: they lie, steal, cheat, beg, and borrow to get whatever it is they want. It's frustrating and frightening. I feel disrespected and inadequate as a parent."

Nick is a brave man who came to me admitting he needed help, which is more than half of any legitimate battle. I met with Nick, established in-home visits, along with telephone and email sessions and helped him and his wife devise a plan to bring their family back together. Within a month, the family was feeling more in concert than ever before. By simply changing the way the family communicated with one another, change came quickly, brought about victory, and had a lasting effect. Nick and his wife learned to talk to their children when things were going well and to set consistent limits for living under their roof. Their relationship with their teenage daughter improved greatly, and the nine-year-old began playing outside and with other friends more regularly.

Jack and Kathy

Jack and Kathy are the parents of three rambunctious children, four-year-old twin boys and a big sister, age 6. Jack and Kathy both work full-time and love being parents.

Before coming to see me, they started to feel that guiding three young children effectively was impossible. Jack and Kathy asked me to teach them how to get their children to do age-appropriate chores, to stop fighting so much with one another, and to obey them.

I worked with Jack and Kathy and their children four times. Following an initial meeting to discuss the Nurtured Heart Approach™ and to ensure that it would fit their situation, I scheduled an in-home visit to observe conditions and interactions, and then met again to devise a plan for the family. After that, we scheduled a follow-up meeting to discuss how things were going.

At the progress meeting, the family reported that the children were excelling. The children were enjoying sharing with each other all of the great qualities which they saw in each other and in their parents. The children were following rules, doing chores, playing nicely and obeying their parents.

Jack and Kathy were amazed at how quickly the troublesome atmosphere had turned around. The house was so pleasant that Jack and Kathy were able to enjoy each other's company a lot more. Bedtime no longer took 3 hours to accomplish. These days, the kids are put in bed and go to sleep! The couple was pleased to learn how easy it was to transform their children and family simply by changing their responses to negativity, changing their perspective, and by being diligent with consequences.

The Nurtured Heart Approach™

How did my family, Nick's family, Jack and Kathy's family and thousands of others turn their families around? They used the Nurtured Heart Approach™. The Nurtured Heart Approach™ is a non-traditional method that teaches people that children want relationship with the adults and other people they love. Children will seek relationship whether they get it for being good or bad. It's up to us as parents to ensure we're giving them fellowship, attention, love and relationship when things are going well and to turn our total attention away from our children when things are not going well.

Parenting Challenging Children with Power, Love and Sound Mind: The Nurtured Heart Approach™ from a Biblical Viewpoint is the Christian version of the Nurtured Heart Approach™. The NHA is a set of strategies — a way of thinking, communicating and interacting — that brings about transformation, balance, inner wealth, inner strength, godliness, gloriousness and greatness to your life. *Parenting with Power, Love and Sound Mind* calls upon your creativity, imagination and artistry to actively recognize, using descriptive language, times when things are going right.

People of all ages want to be valued, appreciated and engaged in relationship and fellowship with others. Intense and challenging children have learned to gain this relational fellowship by *mis*behaving. Following NHA guidelines, you'll be asked to apply positive fellowship and relational comradeship when things are going well, to pull back your relational power and comradeship when things are not going well, and to administer an unceremonious and neutral "reset" whenever rules are broken.

By emotionally applauding the genuine and truthful moments when children are showing good character by displaying wise choices, playing quietly, and not breaking the rules, you can transform them. In this way, they learn to use their God-given skills, talents and abilities in wise and productive ways, creating success and peace in all aspects of their lives.

You'll learn how to master communication skills and timing that will transform your child into the person he was destined by God to be. You'll also learn to skillfully maneuver negative situations every time so that your child is pulled out of the downward spiral and redirected toward success. And you'll learn how to discipline in a manner that uses a "reset" or "time-out." This is not your mother's or your grandmother's "time-out," but an improved way of using a very brief span of time that feels like a true consequence. The new "time-out" is a means to get your child to step out of the negative cycle and allow her to gain self-control and move on to her next successful moment.

If you're thinking at this point that the NHA is too easy because I haven't mentioned spankings and other harsh methods, please stay with me. This approach is scripturally sound and it's relentless when delivered correctly. It won't look a thing like traditional methods because it's far better. It doesn't bring temporary change — it brings lifelong transformation!

Parenting Challenging Children with Power, Love and Sound Mind: The Nurtured Heart Approach™ from a Biblical Viewpoint is for Everyone

Howard Glasser first developed the NHA system for children and teens who are designated "difficult," "challenging" or "intense." It has been shown to work well with children who have been previously diagnosed with Attention Deficit Hyperactivity Disorder, Oppositional Defiant Disorder, Pervasive Developmental Disorder, Autism Spectrum Disorders, Bi-Polar Disorder, Anxiety, Depression, Phobias, Emotional Disturbance and many other disorders, as well as everyday challenges.

The method has also been successful with children who display any of the following behaviors or characteristics: temper tantrums, bed wetting, alcohol and drug abuse, sexual promiscuity, poor social skills, disrespect, strong-will, low self-esteem, sibling rivalry, poor impulse control, inability to focus, anger and defiance issues, challenges to authority, feelings of being misunderstood, stubbornness, struggling in school, truancy, being a "loner," and many other challenging issues.

As time goes on and the popularity of the approach grows, we've discovered that the program produces outstanding results with "marginal" and "average" children, too. Parents who use the approach at home with a difficult child begin to see their "average, easy-to-manage" child blossom further right under their noses; these children, too, begin to truly flourish. In fact, relationships improve across the board. So this book will help you take communication and interaction with all of your children to deeper, more profound mental and emotional levels. It doesn't matter if your child is extremely intense, is challenging, or is one who follows the rules and goes with the flow — all will benefit from your use of the techniques outlined here.

What Does A *Nurtured Heart Approach™* Home Look Like?

Picture a home where everyone gets up in the morning without a fuss and brushes their teeth, combs their hair, and puts on clean clothes. Everyone has completed their homework, breakfast is a breeze, shoes and socks are on and everyone is out the door on time. Visualize a home where yelling, nagging, lecturing and spankings are replaced with laughter and kind words about one another. Sharing is the norm, helping with chores is part of the family plan, and bed-time is a painless event. Teens come home at curfew and make wise choices when they're away. When you visit a store, you don't have to worry about temper tantrums in the aisles or screaming fits because your child can't have the gum that's staring her in the face. You can walk in and near the toy section without meltdowns. Your children have more quality friendships and you get time to yourself. Bedrooms are neat, children pick up after themselves and homework gets done without a fight. Your house is filled with the love and peace of God.

A home invested in this model looks different for everyone because everyone has different needs and wants. But one thing is certain: if you implement *Parenting Challenging Children with Power, Love and Sound Mind: The Nurtured Heart Approach™ from a Biblical Viewpoint* in your home, you will succeed beyond your wildest dreams!

Believe in Miracles — With *Parenting Challenging Children with Power, Love and Sound Mind: The Nurtured Heart Approach™ from a Biblical Viewpoint* They Happen!

If you bought this book to help you with a particularly trying child, you're probably already worn out and have felt like giving up at times. But take heart; you didn't give up and you **can** create the family you want. By the power of God, a miracle can occur in your family. You have enough love for your child that you bought this book. You are obviously passionate about improving your family situation and good at finding resources and solutions. You're an agent of change and faith. God shows the way; simply walk in it and be blessed — and be a blessing!

As a Solution-Focused Brief Family Therapist, I always use The Miracle Question. Developed by Insoo Kim Berg and colleagues at the Brief Family Therapy Center in Milwaukee, Wisconsin, the Miracle Question is designed to create a shift in perception — from problem-oriented thinking to solution-oriented thinking.

Before reading the chapters ahead, take a moment and close your eyes. Picture what your family would look like if a miracle happened today. Close your eyes, get comfortable, forget the world around you and envision what your family, your child, and you would look like if everything were perfect. How would it feel? Taste? Smell? Look? Sound? What would your child be doing? What would you be doing? Where would you be? Where would your child be?

Now, ask yourself: what small step can I take today to put my miracle vision into action? Be specific.

How this Book is Organized

This volume is the Christian version of *Transforming the Difficult Child: The Nurtured Heart Approach*™ (NHA), originally developed by Howard Glasser, MA of Tucson, Arizona. Inside, you'll learn the basic strategies and techniques of this parenting method and social/emotional curriculum, including the Scriptures upon which they are based. You can then put the knowledge you gain to work by completing the "Questions for Reflection" at the end of every chapter. You can do the exercises individually, as a couple, or in a group.

I organized the book in an easy-to-read way that allows you to follow along as though I'm teaching it to you in-person at one of my seminars. The book is broken into sections. The first section will discuss the foundational concepts the approach is built. The next section will discuss the transformation of your parenting power. After we have clearly looked at your parenting style, we will move to transforming the way you view your child or teen. Once these areas are in perspective, we will spend time transforming communication and interaction. After we have mastered those areas, we will move to the section about transforming limit-setting and consequences. Finally, we will transform school and beyond for our children and teens and revel in the sweet joy of victory!

As a teacher, I believe you shouldn't put any new parenting approach into action until you know the bones upon which it is built. As soon as you're confident that you understand the fundamental information, we'll move on to the actual tools, techniques and methods that you'll use with your family and in all other relationships that you want to transform and bless.

Chapter Summary

To summarize, *Parenting Challenging Children with Power, Love and Sound Mind: The Nurtured Heart Approach from a Biblical Viewpoint* is the Christian version of parenting derived from the non-religion based Nurtured Heart Approach™ created by Howard Glasser, M.A.. This approach is used in hundreds of thousands of homes and schools internationally with tremendous results and success. Although the approach was originally created to work with difficult children, it is useful for children of all intensity levels and will help every child flourish beyond normal capabilities. It is a way of thinking, interacting and communicating with children and being present with them when things are going well, and not giving fellowship, relationship or presence to children when things are not going well. It also provides sound structure and consequences when children disobey a rule. The approach can be used by anyone in any situation. It will yield amazing transformational results when used correctly. Remember, "Nothing is impossible with God." (Mark 10:12)

Questions for Reflection

1. Are you truly ready to begin making changes in your family today? Real change means hard work, determination, learning and doing things differently. What makes you certain you are ready?
2. What will you do to sustain those changes?
3. Share in a journal, or with someone you trust, all of **your** current skills, talents and abilities that make you unique.
4. Share in a journal, or with someone you trust, all of **your child's** current skills, talents and abilities that make your child unique.
5. What parenting approach are you using now? How has it been helpful? Unhelpful?
6. Start thinking about building an action plan today to develop your "miracle family." Start small and grow from there. Be specific, realistic and give yourself a time-line for each goal, so you can track your progress.

Prayer for Today

Lord God, help me to read this book with the eyes of my heart. I submit my parenting style to You today and ask for Your direction as I move forward. Parenting is hard work and it's an emotional journey. I ask for forgiveness for any area in which I have inappropriately guided my child. I seek Your Divine guidance as I try to lead in ways that honor You. Fill me with Your Holy Spirit, direct my thoughts, and bring me into abundant blessing, peace and joy as I move forward on this journey. I pray this in Your precious Name, Jesus. Amen.

FOUNDATIONAL CONCEPTS

This section of the book is pivotal, as it describes Howard Glasser's fundamental principles of the Nurtured Heart Approach™. Please read, re-read and refer to it often, as it is the foundation upon which the entire methodology is based.

Chapter 1:
You are a Parent with Power, Love and Sound Mind!

"For God did not give us a spirit of timidity, but of power, of love and of self-discipline (sound mind.)" (2 Timothy 1:7)

"No one has yet realized the wealth of sympathy, the kindness and generosity hidden in the soul of a child. The effort of every true education should be to unlock that treasure." (Emma Goldman)

Welcome to *Parenting Challenging Children with Power, Love and Sound Mind: The Nurtured Heart Approach™ from a Biblical Viewpoint!* I'm honored and privileged to take this journey with you. This program will transform your family. It will help you passionately and truthfully celebrate the children and teens in your life. It will also provide you with a healthier outlook toward the circumstances and people in your world.

Before we begin, I want to express my sincere gratitude to you for being a parent who seeks transformation in your child, who wants God's best for your child, and who is dedicated to *Parenting with Power, Love and Sound Mind.* Yes! I want you to understand that you are a parent who is filled with power, love and sound mind. Parents who raise children with power have a sense of fearlessness and robust energy as they pursue success for their child. Powerful, devoted parents are change agents for their family. Tellingly, knowledgeable parents recognize that their authority comes only from God and from their reliance on Him.

Parents who raise children wisely are filled with compassion, dedication and a true sense of unconditional love for their children. Again, these parents realize that love comes first from God to all of us. His unconditional love for us allows us to model ourselves after Him and to offer unconditional love to our children.

Finally, parents who oversee their children with a sound mind (self-discipline) do so with strength, courage, commitment and faith. All are supplied by our God who cares for us deeply, graciously and mercifully.

You are a parent who parents with power, love and sound mind. You want success for your child, and you are faith-filled, kind and brave, although never perfectly so (there was only one perfect Man). This book will deepen your ability to communicate and interact with your child or teen. It will give you simple methods to transform your children's inner being by increasing their ability to tap into the fountain of life within them that comes from God.

You may be reading this book because things are going great and you want to build upon the foundation you have established. If so, I applaud your quest for continuing growth and knowledge.

If you're reading this because you notice things are starting to get a little rough at home in the parenting department and you realize it's time to get your house in order before it gets beyond your control, you're already wise and powerful.

And if you've chosen this book because you're at wit's end and your child is an eleven on a scale of one to ten in the intensity department, you're understandably broken, worn out, out of options and not sure what to do next. Congratulations for using your last ounce of energy to dive into this book. You have a warrior spirit and will win the war.

As a parent, your eyes are always on the prize and your prize is the well-being of your child. You're diligent, courageous and focused enough to try something new. You want to grow, heal and transform your family. Take heart! God is a rewarder (Hebrews 11:6) to those who diligently seek him.

2 Peter 1:2-8 assures those who know Jesus Christ that they have everything they need for "life and godliness" through His power. I believe living a Godly life means honoring God in all we do. By applying *Parenting with Power, Love and Sound Mind* you will lead and nurture more effectively with these virtues more active and apparent in your life and home. *Parenting with Power, Love and Sound Mind* will help you create a home environment filled with goodness, knowledge, self-control, perseverance, kindness and love and it will enable your children to become more team spirited and cooperative.

"Grace and peace be yours in abundance through the knowledge of God and of Jesus our Lord. His divine power has given us everything we need for life and godliness through our knowledge of Him who called us by His own glory and goodness. Through these He has given us His very great and precious promises, so that through them you may participate in the divine nature and escape the corruption of the world caused by evil spirits. For this very reason, make every effort to add to your faith goodness; and to goodness, knowledge; and to knowledge self-control; and to self-control, perseverance; and to perseverance godliness; and to godliness, brotherly kindness; and to brotherly kindness, love. For if you possess these qualities in increasing measure, they will keep you from being ineffective and unproductive..."
(2 Peter 1:2-8)

Parenting in this Manner is Contrary to Traditional Approaches

"And let us consider how we may spur one another on toward love and good deeds." (Hebrews 10:24)

As you'll discover, *Parenting with Power, Love and Sound Mind* is contrary to many teachings you've learned from other parenting venues. Most approaches tell parents to discipline their children and teach the lesson at the moment misbehavior occurs. But consider: children go into fight-or-flight mode and are not able to absorb a lesson when they're under duress. Your pearls of wisdom remain unheard. To make matters worse, your children learn that your power is totally focused on them when they are misbehaving. Because children crave relationship, they'll unconsciously begin to act out more to receive relationship from you.

So, in essence, traditional parenting tools present three problems:
- they boost and invigorate negative behavior by giving it power and attention;
- they strip away success by not sharing all the amazing qualities and behaviors they see in kids;
- they deliver inconsistent, blurred consequences.

In *Parenting with Power, Love and Sound Mind,* the emphasis goes to the moments when things are going well and there is a de-emphasis on the times when things are going haywire. In a nutshell, positive fellowship and relationship happens when things are going right. There is no longer a need for nagging, warnings, lectures or behavioral modification. A brief time-out or "reset" is all that is needed. You will heap on lots of positive force when things are running smoothly and extinguish power and relationship when things are not up-to-snuff.

The techniques and tools of this system of communication and interaction have been around since the foundations of the earth were formed. *Parenting with Power, Love and Sound Mind* is based on biblical principles of loving others as yourself (Leviticus 19:18), disciplining (teaching) children out of that same spirit of love (Proverbs 3:12) and keeping a positive perspective even in times of trials and tribulations (Philippians 4:4-9, James 1:12-17). Remember what King Solomon said:

"What has been will be again, what has been done will be done again; there is nothing new under the sun. Is there anything of which one can say, 'Look! This is something new?' It was here already, long ago; it was here before our time." (Ecclesiastes 1:9-11)

Parenting with a Warrior Spirit

"Be on your guard; stand firm in the faith; be men of courage; be strong. Do everything in love." (1 Corinthians 16:3-4)

Today's parents must have the attitude that they are fighting for their children's lives and leading the way as warrior-like beings. The modern family is under attack as never before. Divorce and remarriage are rampant. Teens, even Christian teens, are struggling with low self-esteem, school issues, behavioral challenges, unhealthy attitudes, risky decisions; and many are feeling misunderstood by their families. The mental health field is teeming with children and teens (not to mention adults) who are suffering from significant emotional and spiritual distress. Medication seems to be the current answer for everything, which is foolish beyond measure. It's time to rise up and lead as a warrior. Take back the image of the family of your dreams! Fight for the strong foundation our future generation needs to thrive!

There's no question in my mind that you need to parent like a warrior because parenting is the hardest job you'll ever have. There are countless challenges and trials in raising a child: sleepless nights when they are babies and teenagers, fevers, school projects due the next day which would normally take a week, and constant prayers for their safety and spiritual path. Parenting is also potentially the most rewarding job you'll ever have. Nothing can warm a heart like the way you feel about your child. As parents we all experience our baby's first smile, steps and words, the first performance in the school play, graduation from high school, following God's plan in faith, and continuing passion for their lives. The Bible says that children are a gift from God and that they bring blessings (Psalm 127:3). Your warrior spirit in parenting will bring about those blessings.

What Does It Mean to Parent as A Warrior?

1. **Fight the Good Fight of Faith** *"But you man of God, flee from all this, and pursue righteousness, godliness, faith, love endurance and gentleness. Fight the good fight of faith." (1Timothy 6:11-12)*

We need to be warriors because God himself told us we would need to fight. Faith is knowing in your heart that what you want or need will come to pass. If you believe that God is your Creator, that He sent Jesus to live and die for you and that His Scriptures are true, you can access this promise for your life. Walk in love and forgiveness, do not doubt, trust God to get you through and provide for you and you will have the desires of your heart.

As parents, we need to "fight the good fight" of faith for our households, our health, our money, and especially for our children and teens. It is our obligation to fight for the protection of the innocent, to fight for this chosen generation and help them live in the light of God. Equally important, we must fight for the health of their character, values, faith, safety and future. Part of fighting the good fight of faith is living as a warrior spirit with regard to your parenting style and standing firm in faith.

2. **Seek peace, but know how to fight skillfully when necessary:** While raising your children and teens, seek love and peace, but know how to fight if a battle comes up that must be fought for them. Be prepared to

sacrifice and train by staying in good mental, physical, emotional and spiritual shape. Keep up to date on strategies for winning. (Ecclesiastes 3:8, Romans 12:18)

3. Never give up. Be persistent: As parents, we must never grow weary in doing good and in ensuring we are doing all we possibly can for our children. Even when the days look dark, be optimistic and stick with the plan.(Galatians 6:9)

"Have faith in God. I tell you the truth, if anyone says to this mountain, "Go throw yourself into the sea," and does NOT DOUBT in his heart but believes in what he says will happen, it will be done for him. Therefore, I tell you, whatever you ask for in prayer, believe that you have received it, and it will be yours. And when you stand praying, if you hold anything against anyone, forgive him ...."
(Mark 11:22-26)

---

4. Never doubt: Your children, teens and circumstances will get better. Believe and receive. Remember, God is bigger than any of our circumstances and will carry you through. Stay strong in the Lord and in your faith. God will give you the strength to overcome and see your child or teen thriving.

5. Take a stand for the spiritual, physical, mental and financial safety of your children: Taking a stand means to courageously and deliberately believe that your guidance matters and that failure is not an option. (Ephesians 6:13-14)

6. Bring the right weapons to battle: God has provided you with limitless help. You already have some great tools in your toolbox that assist you in parenting. Take the tools you already have and supplement them with what you will learn here to achieve mastery over your parenting style. (Ephesians 6: 10-18)

7. Seek wisdom: *"If any of you lacks wisdom, he should ask God, who gives generously to all without finding fault, and it will be given to him." (James 1:5)*

To lead as a warrior, you must have wisdom that can only come from

God. Ask him and receive His big-hearted and free gift.

8. **Trust God:** *"Trust in the Lord with all your heart and lean not on your own understanding; in all your ways acknowledge him, and he will make your paths straight." (Proverbs 3:5-6)*

   Know too that leading with a warrior spirit will require you to trust in the Lord and not look to yourself for all the answers. Talk to God, ask Him what to do, and follow His path, even if it is contrary to your senses.

9. **Win the battle:** *"The father of a righteous man has great joy; he who has a wise son delights in him. May your father and mother be glad; may she who gave birth to you rejoice." (Proverbs 23: 24-25)*

   The end result of leading your family with a warrior spirit is having a child who is a true blessing to you and others.

The Battle Plan:
Four Guiding Principles for Parenting with Power, Love and Sound Mind

To begin *Parenting with Power, Love and Sound Mind* you need to study and memorize the battle plan set before you. These crucial concepts are the essential components to creating change in your home and winning the battle. Please read, review, re-review and deeply internalize these principles until you're confident you have them in your heart (spirit) and soul.

1. Engage in fellowship with the pure expression of God's Love:

"The Lord God said, It is not good for the man to be alone.
I will make a helper suitable for him." (Genesis 2:18)

God created us to be in relationship with Him and others. God gave Eve to Adam because He knew Adam needed a partner, a friend and a soul mate. We are no different: God created us to be social creatures. The whole basis of *Parenting with Power, Love and Sound Mind* recognizes this truth. Relationship is critical for every human being. We will all seek relationship, fellowship, love and attention from one another and from God. Our children, especially, need and want our time, love and attention and will get it any way they can, through good or bad behavior. The relationship and fellowship you have with your children and teens is what makes or breaks them spiritually and emotionally. The entire book rests on understanding and embracing this first principle.

Parenting with Power, Love and Sound Mind will show you how to engage and connect with your children whenever things are going well. When they're sitting quietly, acknowledge it; when they're just being, acknowledge it, when they're doing even a little of what you require of them, acknowledge the goodness they are displaying in that moment. Don't miss a single opportunity to share something that is right, good and proper about your child or teen.

2. Courageously and valiantly create, cultivate, acknowledge and value positive interactions, behaviors and displays of character:

Relentlessly and strategically pull your child into a new pattern of achievement. Notice every feeling or action, large or small, which you deem an accomplishment. Deliberately share your child's success with him or her using descriptive, positive, truthful language. Continually flood your child with your knowledge of their victories. If your child is being peaceful, responsible, a team player, cooperative, managing their emotions well, let them know exactly what they are doing right so they learn from your positive acknowledgment and want to do it again to stay in positive fellowship with you.

The average child sleeps 8-12 hours in every 24-hour period. During the rest of the time, you have numerous opportunities to cheer your child's positive choices and behavior. Whenever anything praiseworthy occurs, notice it with an expressive, animated narrative. In doing this, you'll become more proficient at noticing wise and appropriate choices and behaviors. Engage in a crusade for **The Endless Pursuit of Positivity!** Positivity connotes the richest sense of being optimistic. Keep your perspective on the positive, constructive, upbeat; on all that is going well at all times.

3. Purposely choose to prune and to refuse to engage in negative, unhealthy and unproductive words, actions and behaviors:

Refuse to be drawn into stimulating, and unintentionally rewarding, your child's bouts of negativity. Don't get sucked into the endless, downward spiraling vortex, a vortex that gives more vitality, greater animation and other unintended "payoffs" to negative behaviors. Don't accidentally reward problems and foster failures by responding with force and relationship; i.e., nagging, lecturing, sermons, yelling. Handle negative behavior by imposing a brief no-drama, non-threatening consequence. Whenever negativity, poor choices or poor behaviors occur, impose a "reset" or time-out that is brief and stops the flow of destructive responses, actions and patterns. Keep the reset brief so your child or teen is quickly placed back in fellowship with you and ushered positively on their way to the next success. *Award power and focus only on your child's successes.*

4. **Purposely, fearlessly and relentlessly establish rules and limits, consistently impose consequences without fear, guilt, intimidation, anger and sadness:**

"I will instruct you (says the Lord) and guide you along the best pathway for your life; I will advise you and watch your progress."
(Psalms 32:8 NLT)

Have clear rules and obvious, consistent consequences for broken rules. Ensure that your children and teens know the rules and let them know what will happen when a rule is broken. Again, be sure to deliver the consequence in a neutral manner. Don't over-stimulate broken rules by going ballistic whenever one is broken. As soon as the consequence is over, immediately begin to inspire and motivate your child to success again. Remember: Your goal is not punishment/consequence; your goal is to encourage your child from accomplishment to accomplishment at a constant pace, communicating to your child that the fabulous, magnificent relationship and power that you share are available only when things are going well.

"Do not merely listen to the Word, and so deceive yourselves. Do what it says." (James 1:22)

These four guiding principles are the foundation upon which the entire approach is built. While reading each chapter, keep in mind these four concepts and the goals written below to master *Parenting with Power, Love and Sound Mind* and proclaim victory for your children and teens!

Winning the Battle:
The Goals of the Four Guiding Principles

Nurture and grow inner wealth and inner strength: Inner wealth and inner strength are placed in each person by God. God fearfully and wonderfully created each and every one of us (Psalm 139:14) and knows all the hairs on our heads (Matthew 10:30). He placed in us the exact makeup of DNA that was necessary for us to fulfill our plan and purpose for our lives. The Divine nature of inner wealth and inner strength increases our ability to deflect conflicts and challenges. People with strong inner wealth and inner strength make choices based on wisdom, knowledge and discernment, allowing for prosperity in all aspects of life. Inner wealth and inner strength is comprised of the qualities, skills, specialties, gifts and talents God has uniquely placed in every being.

Impart godliness, gloriousness and greatness into the world: God-given inner wealth and inner strength is a personal, dynamic and increasing sense of limitless possibilities including: peace, love, joy, selflessness, faith and wellbeing that is then extended to all humanity as one meets and greets others and contributes to the world.

As parents, it is our responsibility to instill inner wealth and inner strength in our children so they live a life filled with godliness, gloriousness and greatness. It is our responsibility to be the biggest influence in their lives and to model what we want them to become.

Children Know

Never underestimate your child. She is continuously watching to figure out how the world works. She forms new impressions daily. As this happens, she begins to interact based on those impressions and assumptions. If your child thinks she'll get more attention and power from a parent when she's misbehaving, she'll misbehave. If she thinks she'll get more attention and power when things are going well, she'll make sure things go well. Children learn very quickly that they have a direct impact on other people's behaviors. ***It's entirely possible that your intense children interpret you as loving and caring for them only when you are nagging, lecturing, yelling or giving a sermon to them.***

Our emotions, our reactions, our level of engagement, and our liveliness are what our children seek. If they get this attention via negative reactions ("no," "stop it," "sit down," "put that away," "go to your room," "behave now," "how many times do I have to tell you"....), that's what they'll do!

On the flip side, if children get attention from positive experiences with their parent, they're likely to seek out that form of engagement ("I appreciated the way you shared your toys with your sister." "You are very kind, thank you for waiting to speak with me until I got off the phone. You are demonstrating patience and courteousness.")

As a parent, you are the expert in your child's life. You get to choose what kind of power you radiate, how you radiate it, and when you radiate it.

Remember: There is No Blame

"Forgetting what is behind and straining toward what is ahead, I press on toward the goal to win the prize for which God has called me heavenward in Christ Jesus." (Philippians 3:14)

If for any reason you're starting to feel condemnation because of the way you have interacted with or addressed your children in the past, please end that "stinking thinking" right now! Don't waste time blaming yourself, your kids, their teachers, or the people who created the upside down methods you were told to use. Every one of these individuals was doing the best they could with the information they had. This includes you! Remember, every day is a new day. Dust off and start anew. Today, you are being handed new tools for your tool box. Go forward *Parenting with Power, Love and Sound Mind* from today on. It doesn't take long to make an amazing change!

Remind yourself that you're the most influential person in your child's life. You are the authority on you, your children and your family. You have a plethora of God-given skills, talents and abilities. You can instill inner wealth, inner strength, godliness and greatness in your child and become their hero!

Consistency is Key

As with every new learning experience, it's important to be consistent. No approach, not even one steeped with God's wisdom, will provide transformation if it is not used with passionate fervor on a daily basis. So be patient, be persistent and have faith that a new way of life filled with the fruits of the spirit is coming. Most importantly, remind yourself not to be casual in your relationship with your child or teen. Press in daily and fervently so you can obtain all of the goodness, mercy and grace that God is offering you every moment of your life.

Tap into your Creativity

Because this approach is counterintuitive, you will be called on to creatively, intelligently and artistically interact with and lead your children. Instead of dealing with problems when they come up, you'll provide the "lesson"/kudos/compliments/positive acknowledgment to your child when they are behaving. When your child is quiet, getting chores done, doing as you asked or behaving in a manner consistent with the values and character qualities you want them to model, you'll creatively and expressively share with them "what is going right."

Rather than providing long, drawn out lectures or warnings when your kids misbehave, you'll simply offer your child or teen a "reset." The reset provides a brief, zero energy span of time — the perception of a consequence. The consequences are solid, unbending and relentless but in no way harsh or severe. The reset is designed to quickly, without fanfare, put the brakes on inappropriate behavior so the child can get beyond it and into the next moment of celebrated success.

The Beauty Within Emerges

The beauty of *Power, Love and Sound Mind* is that it gives children and teens so much truthful, delicious energy and information about themselves while they're doing something right, that they decide it's best not to do things wrong. As you practice the approach, you'll see the results with your own eyes. You'll watch your children emerge from their cocoons in magnificent ways, revealing beauty and skills that before were hidden.

You'll see them make wise choices at home, at school and in the social arena. You will see them being calm, kind, making more friends and expressing love, power and sound mind in healthy ways.

Timetable for the approach to work

Immediate results are possible. As soon as a child hears and genuinely begins to **internalize** what you're saying and feeling, change begins. And since we use conversation to artfully guide the interaction, five minutes a day is all it takes. The five minutes is simply divided up into ten-second intervals of recognition, genuine acknowledgement (truthful recognition) and thirty or more descriptions of what was wonderful about what occurred.

I suggest that you diligently soak in the new positive perspective you will be asked to adopt, and practice each of these techniques (which I will later define); active recognition, experiential recognition, proactive recognition and creative recognition, for a few days or a week until you feel you've learned them. Your goal is to finish each technique individually until you feel confident and secure about using it and it becomes more or less ingrained. As soon as you've mastered all of the strategies, start combining them and use them at a more advanced level.

After you have learned the communication strategies in the following chapters, you'll graduate to limit setting, consequences and boundaries. While learning these philosophies, avoid as much negative interaction as possible. If your child breaks a rule, simply tell them to "reset" (or any other appropriate word on which you decide on that stops the negative behavior). As soon as they show a single sign of discontinuing the negative behavior, let them know the reset is over, have them right any wrongs they may have committed, and welcome them back into success with positive, descriptive fellowship and recognition for their achievement. If this seems foreign to you right now, that's okay. It takes time to feel comfortable doing something different. Until you master the mindset and philosophy of the approach and know the recognitions in the following chapters, keep disciplining the way you're used to, but do so with as little discussion, emotion, energy or relationship as possible. Experiment with keeping the consequence simple and short, so it passes quickly and all of you can move on to the next moment of success.

Realistically, you can expect full implementation of *Parenting with Power, Love and Sound Mind* in about one month.

Be Patient with Yourself and Your Child

"By perseverance the snail reached the ark." (Charles Haddon Spurgeon)

Remain confident that results will happen at the right pace for your child. It takes time to learn a new way of living; change isn't easy. Give yourself and your child credit for each step you take toward mastering the approach, and recover quickly when you backslide. You'll get to the transformation sooner rather than later as long as you don't beat yourself up when you have a setback.

Do Not Fear but Trust in God

"Have patience with all things, but chiefly have patience with yourself.
Do not lose courage in considering your own imperfections, but instantly
set about remedying them — every day begin the task anew."
(Saint Francis De Sales)

Take a deep breath, relax and enjoy this new adventure. I'm confident you'll be thrilled as the children and teens in your life soak up *Parenting with Power, Love and Sound Mind* and convert themselves into leaders, filled with God's character and abundance.

I've worked with many families. Countless interviews with parents have confirmed that fear is a nasty emotion to have when running a household. Fear comes in many forms: fear of failure, fear that you are not an adequate parent, fear of harm, fear your child may stop walking with the Lord and instead will follow the ways of the world, or fear that their choices may lead them to destruction. We need to remember that God tells us not to fear and to rely on Him in everything we do. This includes parenting. As Barbara J. Winter puts it "When you come to the edge of all you know and are about to step off into the darkness of the unknown, faith is knowing one of two things will happen: there will be something solid to stand on — or you will be taught how to fly!"

I'm an avid proponent of Christian meditation. Christian meditation is the process of quieting your mind and concentrating on God and Scripture

(Psalm 1:1-3, Jeremiah 17:7-8). Throughout the Bible, Jesus and others meditated regularly, spending quiet time with God. Meditation quiets our minds from thinking about the past and the future and allows us to simply enjoy the present moment. One of my favorite guided meditations talks about removing fear from your life by literally picturing every care you have and then getting a clear image of yourself taking that care to the cross, nailing it there and turning away to leave it solely with Jesus. I encourage you, if fear plagues you, to take a moment and do what 1 Peter 5:7 says: Cast your cares on the Lord and know that He will handle everything for you. God created the world; he can fix your problems. God answers prayers of the righteous and wants you to live in abundance, joy and peace. So stop worry, misery and doubt in their tracks. Leave it to Jesus!

Consider the words of these passages of Scripture:

"Cast all your anxiety on Him because He cares for you." (1 Peter5:7)
"You will be kept in perfect peace in him whose mind is steadfast, because he trusts in you. Trust in the Lord forever, for the Lord, the Lord, is the Rock eternal." (Isaiah 26:3-4)

"Do not be anxious about anything, but in everything, by prayer and petition, with thanksgiving, present your requests to God. And the peace of God, which transcends all understanding, will guard your hearts and your minds in Christ Jesus." (Philippians 4:6-7)

God is bigger than your fears. He answers the prayers of the righteous and wants you to know His peace. As you live out these promises be bold and, by the power of God, take loving, effective control of your family situation.

Transformation

"People of ordinary ability sometimes achieve outstanding success because they don't know when to quit. Most folks who succeed do so because they are determined to."
(George E. Allen)

As mentioned above, parenting an intense or challenging child through *Power, Love and Sound Mind* brings transformation — a radical alteration in his or her character, values and appearance. When children live in an environment that treats them as "outsiders" or "adversaries," they form negative impressions of the world and of themselves. And these impressions are enforced every time they receive relationship and connection through adversity. Traditional parenting methods often confuse or aggravate the situation because the child or teen mistranslates the harsh consequence *as a reward.* It is better to have a terrible relationship than none at all.

The purpose of *Parenting with Power, Love and Sound Mind* is to let your child or teen know that there is no genuine relationship in negative or adversarial behavior. Real relationship can only be planted in "good soil" (positive behavior). Positive behavior builds trust; negative behavior destroys it.

In a series of well-designed steps, success is created by actively and accurately acknowledging progress and by laying down a foundation of easy-to-understand limits and boundaries. When the challenging child internalizes the deliciousness of success and realizes that the only way to gain relationship is to follow the rules through trustworthy, positive behavior, he or she stops mistranslating the word "relationship" and begins to honor his or her inner wealth — and everyone else's! A transformation takes place and a happier, more content child emerges.

The objective is to create transformation in your child help him recognize moments when he has acted positively, when he has shared his inner wealth and inner strength and greatness, godliness and gloriousness.

Questions for Reflection

1. Do you think you can parent with a warrior spirit and fight the good fight of faith to win? What characteristics in you make you a warrior parent? How have you fought for your children and teens in the past? Are you prepared to rely on God as you continue to stand up for them?

2. When do you radiate the most liveliness? Bedtime? Dinner time? Homework time? Chore time? When things are going well?

3. Think of as many scenarios as possible in which you can radiate positive relationship and delightful fellowship with your children and teens. Write them down. Even the simplest of times count.

4. Name some ways you can begin to create success in your child today.

5. What is your default setting? Is your perspective positive or negative most of the time? Try to engage in positivity all of the time.

6. One day as you go about your business, notice all of the wonderful characteristics of people and give them descriptive feedback. Note how you feel at the end of the day. Dedicate yourself to providing genuine appreciation and praise to as many people as you can every day.

7. How can you use the knowledge you have learned in this chapter to increase your parenting skills?

8. What are some ways you currently parent that you are proud of and wish to continue?

9. Take your Bible and find other Scriptures that confirm *Parenting with Power, Love and Sound Mind* is consistent with God's Word. Write them down for future use.

Prayer for Today

Father, give me the strength to emphatically saturate my child with successes. Help me to radiate and accept only positive fellowship and relationship with my child. Give me the know-how to learn, perfect, navigate, and increase my creative bent so I can do whatever it takes to win the battle and make sure my child experiences success after success.

God, thank You for teaching me who You are, who I am through Jesus Christ and for giving me the Holy Spirit to guide and direct my steps as I parent my child. Thank You, that through You I am more than a conqueror and that I have every need met according to the glorious riches in Christ Jesus. Thank You for helping me recognize that I am not a perfect parent and that I do not have to be one. I have You, Jesus and the Holy Spirit working and living with me to make me the best parent I can be. I am already perfect when viewed through the eyes of Christ. Help me to continue to see myself as You see me. You see me as a child of God with gifts, talents and abilities that You placed in me to do good works. I submit my life to You Lord. I pray this in the Name of Jesus. Amen.

TRANSFORMING YOUR PARENTING POWER

This section helps you to explore the kind of parent God is. You will discover some of your own parenting styles and how to take them from successful to sensational. You will also explore the importance of guarding your heart, mind and words.

Chapter 2:
God: The Only Perfect Parent

"What God is to the world, parents are to their children." (Philo)

Now that we have learned the foundational principles of *Parenting with Power, Love and Sound Mind*, it's imperative to tackle an assessment of your current child-rearing ideologies and ensure that they're aligned with the Word of God and with this approach. In this chapter we will fully realize that God is the only perfect parent. He is all encompassing love, majestic and righteous. The Great I AM is all-knowing, all-powerful and ever-present in our lives. He is filled with mercy, grace, forgiveness, compassion, patience, watchfulness and knowledge beyond our own understanding. God is also just, fair, slow to anger, a provider of boundaries, structure, limits and rules for those He loves. Our Creator has given us the gifts of Jesus Christ and the Holy Spirit to help us successfully navigate the world in every area of life. We learn a lot when we use God as an example of how to be a magnificent parent. We learn to take hold of the inheritance we have through Jesus Christ and the direction and guidance of the Holy Spirit to be the best parents we can possibly be.

Below you'll find a number of stories from parents who were seeking change. They met their challenges and turned their families around. While reading their accounts, check your own parenting style to determine if your parenting approach is well-managed and thoughtful as you raise and care for your children. If you find yourself out of control in any area, ask God for forgiveness and ask the Holy Spirit to give you a positive, helpful new direction, then move on to the next moment of success and leave the past behind. Remember, *Parenting with Power, Love and Sound Mind* believes that victorious child-rearing includes more liveliness, power and fellowship when things are going well and zero attention when things are going awry, coupled with consistent limit setting and boundaries.

I'm here to remind you, every step of the way, that God cares about you, loves you, and wants the best for you and your family. He will only give you as much as you will be able to handle. He knew exactly what he was doing when he blessed you with your children. Through faith and reliance on Him, He will do good works in you. Now let's take a deeper look at who God really is and how He should be viewed as well as how His values and characteristics parallel *Parenting with Power, Love and Sound Mind*.

God is Love

Pastor Lee Wilson, Youth Minister of Abundant Life Christian Center, shared a humorous story about what all too many parents teach their children. Parents teach us to pray: *"You'd better pray that stain comes out"*, *"I pray you have a child just like you."* Parents teach us about our future: *"I am going to knock you into the middle of next week."* They teach us about preparation: *"Wear your clean underwear in case you get into an accident."* They teach us to count: *"I will give you to the count of three!"* (Abundant Life Christian Center Marriage Enrichment Class on CD 2009).

While Pastor Lee's account is knee-slapping funny, at times we probably don't have to walk far to be on common ground with the above-quoted parents. The only perfect parent is God. As Christians, it's important to understand the love of God in order to appreciate stellar parenting.

In scripture, agape is said to be the highest form of love. By definition, "Agape is love which is of and from God, whose very nature is love itself." "God is love." (1 John 4:8) But God doesn't merely love as an act in itself; He *is* love itself. Everything God does flows from His love and affection toward us. But it's important to realize that God's love is not sappy, sentimental, selfish, sexual, conditional or fickle. God loves because it is His nature and the faultless expression of His being. He loves the unlovable and the unlovely (that's all of us!) not because we deserve to be loved, but because it is His nature to love us, and since God is not a liar, He must be true to His nature and character.

Agape love from God calls us to love others sacrificially. Sacrificial love is not based on how we feel about others, but on a determined act of the will. It is a joyful resolve to put the welfare of others above our own. It is a love that is patient and kind, it is not envious or arrogant, it is not rude or self-seeking, it is slow to anger, rejoices in truth and bears, believes and hopes in all things (1 Corinthians 13:1-13). We love not to receive accolades and acceptance from others, but out of love and obedience to God.

But this manifestation of love is far from natural to humans. Because of our fallen nature, we're incapable of **perfectly** reproducing agape love. When we do manage to love as fully as God loves, it's because what we give passes through us from its true Source: God. This is the love which "has been poured out in our hearts through the Holy Spirit given to us" when we became His children (Romans 5:5). (www.gotquestions.com)

As parents, we must remember to love our children without expectation of receiving anything in return. To follow God's example, we must love our children without limit even when they are unlovely and we must love them with God's brand of love.

God is Love and Justice

In *Parenting with Power, Love and Sound Mind* we need to remember to love our children and guide them with consistent limits, rules and structure. God is a God of love and justice so He will discipline those He loves in order to keep them on the right path. When discipline is necessary, it's important to follow the example of God by imposing a quick consequence, offering up forgiveness, restoring fellowship and moving on to the next moment of success.

What is Your Perspective of God?

Do you see God as a grandfatherly type, sitting on His rocking chair on the porch? If so, you may believe that God is detached from everyone and simply allows life to go on without His active involvement.

Or do you see God as a police officer or a drill sergeant? If so, perhaps God is, to you, all about punishment and harsh, legalistic ways. People who believe this way about God tend to walk through life guilt-ridden. If you're among them, you never feel quite good enough and you may live in constant fear of dire outcomes.

Some people see God as a puppeteer and themselves as His puppet. These folks view God as being in control of everything they do. They take no personal stake or responsibility in the way they navigate life.

Another way that people view God is through the lens of their own experience. A perspective of God based on personal experience with one's own mother and father or other authority figures in your life is dangerous because we ascribe human characteristics to God and don't see Him in the fullness of His divinity.

It's nice to know that God is none of the above. God is not an all-or-nothing God. He is perfect and adheres to a righteous, loving structure. Everything He does is in our best interest and to increase our reliance on Him. Jesus regularly referred to God as "Abba," best translated in our language as "daddy." God is not distant; He is available to us, caring and protective, concerned about our needs and He wants to see us prosper in all areas of our lives.

Allow God to show you His immensity and true nature. Drink in all that He is and all that He has to offer. As a parent, you'll need to draw on the strength of God at all times, especially when you feel weak and weary. You're expected to be the strength in your own household and to reflect the true majesty and power of God. As parents, we act the most like God when we see our newborn child for the very first time. We look at the newly born little bundle of joy with wonder, awe and amazement and inspect him closely from head to toe. We also know nothing about this little person — his potential, his gifts, his desires are mysteries — but we love him anyway with all of our hearts. This is love that loves because of the mere presence of our precious newborn and it is the closest we come to the kind of love God has for us.

God as a Parenting Example

We can't be perfect parents, or have all of God's attributes, but we can take some of His ways and make them our own. Before you engage with your children, visualize yourself addressing them with power, love and sound mind the way God does (with love, forgiveness and a structure that includes consequences). This is discipline! Love your children unconditionally; provide them with boundaries and then share with them all of the qualities you see in them that bring you blessing, peace and joy. Lead with compassion and watchful eyes. Be who you are; be truthful with your children. Persistently and consistently shower them with blessings _and_ limits. Be close enough to your children that you know the inside scoop on their friends, the music they listen to, what they watch on television and their favorite activities and hobbies. Be an example through your own actions and words.

Extreme to Extraordinary: Parenting Transformations

"It's important to let our kids know we are aware of our inadequacies. Tell them. You have nothing to lose in honestly admitting to them that you didn't do everything correctly as a parent. The admission may be the key to opening communication and beginning the process of healing your relationships with your kids."
(Stephen Arterburn and Jim Burns, <u>When Love is not Enough</u>)

I've seen a wide variety of parenting styles in my profession. As you read the stories, please note that names and certain details have been changed to protect the confidentiality and privacy of the individuals involved. I'm sharing my thoughts on extreme parenting styles because they are so prevalent and occur every day in many households. The parents you'll meet below took the time and effort to make substantial changes in the way they live and emerged triumphant. The examples will help you determine if you're involved in anything yourself as a parent that needs to be reined in. If you are, I want to make it clear that I am casting no blame or judgment on you. Some of these methods are "prevailing wisdom" (as opposed to Godly wisdom). Every one of the families responsible for these extreme examples are filled with love for one another and have their own special thoughts and actions that make them valuable assets to the kingdom of God and to the communities in which they live. Remember, each family here experienced a transformation and you can, too. I pray these stories bring you hope.

As parents, we're all doing the best we can under complicated circumstances. So if you see yourself in any of these examples, take heart that God can and will help you move toward different outcomes that will bless you and your family.

The Super-Spiritual Parent: This parent makes everything about God and Holiness. Although it's vitally important to love God and serve Him, not everything is about God at all times.

A young pastor once told me a story about a seminary friend. The friend was so out of touch with life that he told his children to ask God's direction for everything they did, including when they went to a soda machine. The man's young son literally would stand in front of the soda machine and say, "If it be the Lord's will, I will have a diet soda. Lord, guide my decision."

Luckily, a wise pastor in the school learned what the young shepherd-in-training was doing with his children and guided him to see that God also gave us the gift of free will. God wants relationship with us; he doesn't want us to be silly fools. It's okay to have fun, laugh and put God out of your thoughts for certain events. It's okay to just go ice skating or enjoy a day at the beach without making it a spiritual event. God knows our hearts. He never leaves our spirits.

The Over-Involved Parent: As the name indicates, this parent is overly involved with their child. While parents are expected to know the whereabouts and safety of their flock, they are not supposed to make decisions for them every time or bail them out of every situation they get themselves into. Over-involved parents create a sense of incompetence, inadequacy, irresponsibility, dependence and fear in their children, which reduces their ability to gather inner wealth and takes away opportunities for them to achieve success on their own.

Katrina

Katrina, a twelve year old middle school student, didn't like to organize herself at school. Her mom talked until she was blue in the face about Katrina becoming more organized. She bought Katrina folders and organized the work within them for her.

But Katrina's own lack of responsibility cost the young lady a passing grade on a major report. Mom demanded a meeting with the teacher because she felt it was the teacher's fault that Katrina had failed. In Mom's eyes, the teacher should have recognized that Katrina had organizational issues and should have personally ensured that Katrina was handling her assignments well. Numerous discussions with the whole class were not good enough.

Now, there is no question that Katrina is deeply loved by her mom. The problem arose because Katrina had Mom fighting her battles and was not being held accountable. Katrina was spiraling into depression and anxiety (right along with her mom) because she wasn't "measuring up" and yet was not being expected to step up and learn a new skill.

I suggested to mom to stop nagging, warning and "doing" and meet Katrina where she was, giving her genuine praise when Katrina was doing something well and leaving the negative alone. She needed to let the consequences of Katrina's actions rain down on her so she could take real control in her life.

My suggestion was hard for mom, but she did it. The result: Katrina quickly learned to do the right thing and realized along the way her own potential for greatness.

Mom needed to learn to let go and give Katrina the reins so she could experience success on her own and develop inner wealth and a sense of accomplishment.

Parents Who Have Given Up or Are Too Busy

This type of parent comes in two forms:

(1) one who has stopped trying to lead or guide because of frustration, anger, disappointment or a sense of failure or loss of control; and

(2) one who is so busy working, socializing or pursuing a hobby that he or she (or they) forget they're the most influential people in their child's life. The children of these parents desperately need them, no matter how the child is acting. Busy parents are easily manipulated and are usually completely unaware that it's going on!

Latoya and Quentin

Latoya, a mother of three children ages 16, 12 and 7 was so addicted to playing a computer game that she forgot about her family. Latoya would go to work, then return home and spend every waking minute on the computer. Her husband, Quentin, worked two jobs and was rarely around.

Both Latoya and Quentin were surprised when they learned from a concerned neighbor that their sixteen-year-old daughter was actively involved in the drug scene. They came into my office wondering what to do. To add to the nightmare, the middle child, Richie, had asked to borrow a credit card to make an online purchase for some sports gear. Quentin had handed him the card without asking for any more information. Not long after, a UPS truck rolled up with a thousand dollars worth of sporting equipment for Richie and two of his "less fortunate" friends!

I helped Latoya and Quentin see that their personal priorities and lack of involvement with their children were not helping them. Latoya and Quentin listened, absorbed my information, and began to interact with their emotionally-starved children. And because they began noticing them and sharing with them, all were back in the game of life and the children blossomed into wonderful people.

Parents Who Give In to Their Children Because of Guilt: Parents who give in to guilt trips are wounded themselves and need help healing. This parent typically comes out of an addiction, an abusive relationship, or may have lost a spouse or feel responsible for an accident or negative life experience that happened to their child. This parent must recognize that the child needs limits and boundaries, not a "yes" every time.

The recovering guilt tripper does not want to hurt his child anymore. He feels the child has experienced too much pain already — possibly because of foolish parental decisions. If a child has been traumatized by an unfortunate event or a difficult lifestyle, he should not get everything for which he asks. For a child to achieve his personal best, he needs a parent who is actively involved and has limits. Sometimes "no" is the best word a child can hear.

Trudy

Trudy is the mother of a fourteen-year-old boy, Tyler. For 12 years Trudy and Tyler lived with a husband and father who was physically, emotionally and verbally abusive. Trudy felt so guilty about keeping her son in that environment for so many years that she said "yes" to everything. "Yes, Tyler could stay home from school. Yes, Tyler could have a cell phone. Yes, Tyler could have $100 jeans on mom's super-tight budget."

Tyler became a raging beast with all kinds of demands that Trudy just could not meet. If he didn't get what he wanted he yelled, threw things and roared until mom finally gave in.

I worked on healing and God's forgiveness with Trudy while she worked on Tyler. Trudy actively acknowledged the times when he was content, appreciated him for behaviors she favored, and shared high verbal energy when he got up to go to school. Tyler began experiencing love and respect for his mother. He saw her as more than just a wallet.

Parents Who Are Friends with Their Children: This type of parent may allow their child and his or her friends to come to the house to drink alcohol and smoke cigarettes. Some may even allow a boyfriend over to have sex. They do this under the misguided belief that, "If they are going to do this, at least I know where they are and that they're safe." This type of parent may also be actively involved with the social scene of the child, dressing similarly, listening to the same music, texting with the child's friends, and participating in all the drama.

Yes, we need to be involved with our children. But we also need to have our own friends, identity and hobbies. Not to mention limits.

Thomas

Thomas, a recently-divorced parent and father of two children, Dustin, age 6 and Mariah, age 14, was having a hard time adjusting to the single life. Thomas found himself drawn to talking with Mariah's friends. He became part of Mariah's crowd. He ended up with a child protective report and a criminal charge of endangering the welfare of a child because one night he allowed the children to watch a pornographic movie and drink wine coolers.

Thomas was a sweet man who loved God but got himself into a bind with a serious error in judgment. Thomas hadn't learned to have a life outside of his children, and became their buddy. To help Thomas, Dustin and Mariah, I had to help Thomas see himself as their authority figure, not their friend, as a person who could have fun with them and share successes with them, but also as someone who needs to put limits and consequences in place for himself and his children.

I'm happy to report the family is now doing very well, is heavily involved with church and that Thomas now runs a weekly support group for Christians overcoming divorce.

Parents Who Are Always Right and Perfectionist Parents : This is the parent who provides "pearls of wisdom" at every turn and doesn't take much time to listen to their children. This parent thinks it's important to share all they can with their child about their behavior, education, choice of friends, skill level and style of dress. This parent knows best and can see no other way.

While it's important to maintain high standards for our children, parents also need to give them room to make their own choices and to have a voice. Children too have feelings, thoughts and dreams. We need to be able to hear them. Children are intuitive, creative and skilled at making lots of decisions. The more you allow them to test and experience the world, the more they'll be able to encounter and grasp God's vision and plan for their lives.

Moses and Samantha

Moses and Samantha owned a small deli in a local city, inherited from Moses' father. Both parents intended to pass it on to their eldest son, fifteen-year-old Micah. The problem was that Micah hated cooking and had no interest in becoming part of the family business. When Micah would tell this to them, they would counsel him on all the reasons he needed to change his mind.

Micah began to loathe his parents. They were constantly nagging, lecturing and warning him about his future. It became so difficult for everyone that Micah ran away and refused to come home. A friend put them in touch with me.

I taught *Parenting with Power, Love and Sound Mind* to the family and helped them to see the need for Micah to be Micah. And as soon as they began to appreciate Micah in his own right and showered him with genuine love and acceptance for his own path, Micah came home.

All has been well since. The last I heard, Micah was a senior in high school and getting ready to go to college to become a veterinarian.

Shawna and Walter

Another form of the perfectionist parent is the one who wants all her children to behave like angels in every situation so that she can present to the world a "squeaky clean" appearance. This is the parent who expects her child to not only play baseball but to be the star player, to be the class valedictorian, or the be lead in the play. Second-best is not acceptable and "A" is the only game.

Shawna and Walter had seven-year-old twins. They were in every activity known to man. Dance, karate, acting, soccer, baseball, creative arts, you name it, the twins were involved. Shawna and Walter wanted their kids to have the best of everything because they felt deprived as children due to of monetary constraints. Shawna and Walter overcame their environments and both became successful doctors. And although their children looked perfect and knew how to do just about everything at a young age, as a family they were not doing well. Their mutually-exclusive schedules disconnected them and took away time for bonding. The children regarded their parents as chauffeurs and struggled with anxiety and depression.

I worked with the family and soon learned that all were quick to point out the negatives of their family members. They were completely consumed by the notion that perfection was the only worthwhile goal.

I helped the family see themselves as God sees them. They are fragile, imperfect, perfectly-loved people who could never achieve perfection on their own, but through Jesus they were people with special skills, talents and abilities that could — and should — be embraced. We got to work nurturing everyone. As a few activities were dropped, they spent more quality time with one another, and were able to actively recognize each other, all of which allowed them to begin living in and enjoying the present moment.

Parenting with Fear and Control: This form of parenting is based on a drill sergeant mentality. Parents who use their authority to control by fear have a hard time showing physical and emotional love and sharing a range of emotions and expressions. In this home, children are compelled to do what they're told, no questions asked. If they fail to obey, there are harsh physical or emotional consequences. This type of parenting tends to paralyze children and make them fearful of authority figures.

Children who grow up in this type of environment typically become either extremely passive or withdrawn, or very aggressive, and regard most situations as adversarial. Children who live in homes with fear and control as the main parenting style suffer from low self-esteem. They tend to lack social and communication skills and have a hard time understanding and expressing emotion.

Parents who work from this mode tend to be very rigid in their thinking and behavior. Certain subjects are taboo, so communication is not open, honest or real. The perceived family leader runs the home and controls the feelings of everyone in the house.

This form of parenting steals success from children. The parents view themselves as the reason for success because they control everything that goes on, as in a dictatorship. Children who grow up in this environment feel disempowered, have little inner wealth because of lack of successes, and receive little praise for their achievements.

Carl and Belinda

Carl and Belinda have three sons. Harold is in first grade, Paul is in fourth grade and Allen is in eleventh grade. Carl and Belinda rarely go out and almost never leave their children with anyone. They control nearly every movement their children make. This includes not allowing Carl's loving and caring mother to have any independent interaction with the children.

I came to know the family because Allen was a "cutter." A cutter is a child that has a difficult time expressing him or herself because of suppressed emotions. One surefire way to remove the emotional pain and find some relief from it is to cause physical harm to his or her body.

Allen cut himself relentlessly when we first met. He used razors, glass, anything he could get his hands on. At times, he would even burn himself. One of the biggest hurdles I had in working with this family was helping them see that their unhealthy rigidity was affecting the entire family.

Carl and Belinda truly loved their children. In fact, they adored them so much that they felt they should shelter them and enforce strict rules. The most recent rule to cause a stir in the house was the "prom rule": Allen could go to the prom but he couldn't go with any of his guy friends, all of whom were eager to go with him as a large rambunctious group. He needed to have a female date because that was tradition.

Carl and Belinda told Allen to "go find a date." Predictably, the pressure of finding a date for a socially isolated young man, even one with charm and brains, caused his emotional turmoil to skyrocket. To stop the emotional pain, Allen decided to take a bottle of Tylenol.

At the hospital, Allen told us he couldn't live like a captive animal anymore. That's when his parents recognized the need for them to change.

It has been well over two years since that incident and I am proud to say the family is thriving. Carl and Belinda did a lot of soul searching about their beliefs and rules. Allen is free of self-injurious behavior and is blossoming into an independent, artistic and creative young man.

Henry and Miranda

Henry and Miranda have been married for many years and have five children ranging in age from 2-17. Henry is the ruler of his castle and expects everyone to do as he says. When Henry comes home he expects the house to be neat and the children to be quiet. If things are not to his satisfaction, Henry screams at the children. He will share his disdain with them and attack their character.

Due to Henry's parenting style, Miranda began compensating for his behavior. Henry would parent with an iron fist; to compensate, Miranda would be extra kind, providing no discipline or structure. The kids were confused, but began manipulating the situation and acting out in a variety of ways. The family came to me when their pre-school asked that one of their children be removed from class due to of an outburst of verbal and physical anger.

Initially, I worked only with Miranda and the children. As time went by and Henry began to trust me, he came to the sessions. He shared that he was raised in a home that didn't tolerate emotional closeness; compliance was all that mattered.

As soon as Henry was able to see the damage he was doing, he softened his approach at home. He slowly began to positively and descriptively share what he saw the children doing that pleased him. Henry's change in perspective allowed Miranda to change hers. She and Henry began to communicate more and work together as a couple instead of working from opposite ends of the spectrum.

Picture of a Successful Parent

Here is a picture of a parent destined to meet with success: a parent who daily interacts with her child, remains teachable, is always learning, behaves and thinks in a balanced manner, is a good role model, always walks in love, forgives continuously, has patience galore, is a skilled teacher and communicator, who guides and encourages with purpose and positive passion and one who possesses characteristics from all of the parents above within reasonable limits. And the most significant characteristic is a heavy reliance on God and His Word.

Video Games Can Help You Become a Better Parent

"Life is 10% of what happens to me and 90% how I react to it."
(John Maxwell)

My children, Savannah and Chandler, can play video games until their eyes pop out of their heads, or until Brian and I tell them to stop and go outside. Both of my children are intense — they enjoy being outside, playing sports, and a host of other physical activities — but when it comes to their video games, they are truly fixated.

When I teach *Parenting Challenging Children with Power, Love and Sound Mind: The Nurtured Heart Approach™ from a Biblical Viewpoint* I ask parents if their children enjoy video games. Almost all say yes. They tell me, even before I ask, that the video games are the one thing that truly captivates their kids and holds their undivided, super-engaged attention.

The reason why super-engagement occurs is that video games make perfect sense emotionally.

- They have very clear and predictable rules;
- There is a whole lot of energy output (sounds, lights and higher scores) for following the rules, and even bigger incentives for complete mastery at every skill level;
- When your child is doing well in the game, he is rewarded at every turn (positive bells and whistles are flowing and it feels good);
- When he makes a mistake the consequence is clear, quick and neutral. He feels the consequence (you can usually hear the "Ahhh, man!" across the room) but then he's immediately ushered back into

the game where he jumps right back into winning. The game keeps him in the NOW. Results can't be manipulated.

The feeling of accomplishment and success in conquering games is significant. It is translated internally as, "I am a success because I defeated this game."

Games make a big deal over success, so the child wants it. Games make very little fuss over missteps, but do provide a brief consequence. So in the world of video games, children become experts at doing things right.

As a parent and as a Nurtured Heart practitioner, I encourage you to borrow the video game strategy and create success for your children in the same way. Give your children lots of incentives (genuine sharing of the truth and positive power and fellowship) when you see things going well. Give them a clear, brief, neutral, zero energy consequence when you see your children doing things that are not in their best interest. The point is to get your children back in the game of doing well as soon as possible and then heaping them with additional positive accolades so they'll seek more of it time after time. In this way, children will begin to use their personal power to succeed in life.

I should note here that I am not a huge proponent of video games. I'm very careful about the games I allow my children to enjoy. Video games should not negate the lifestyles you want to promote in your child's life. The sole point I make regarding video games is that children become proficient with playing them because they make perfect sense logically and emotionally. So it might help you just to carry the video game analogy in your in your mind to help you remember to keep consequences brief and to celebrate positive behavior with relationship interaction that resonates with your child and lets him or her know that what he or she did was great.

Dust Off and Forgive Yourself

I'll end this chapter the same way I started it: by agreeing with you that there is no perfect parent except God. You'll experience regrets as a parent and you'll make mistakes. No one expects anything else, including God! Just dust yourself off, forgive yourself, and know that perfection is not, and never has been, an achievable goal. God created you the way you are and He accepts you as you are, warts and all. Embrace and love yourself exactly where you are and for the skills that you do have. Ask God to forgive you for past mistakes. His mercy is new every morning, so allow yourself a clean slate with each new moment and seek His guidance as you proceed (1 John 1:9). Remember to embrace each new opportunity as still another occasion to create success.

Chapter Summary

This chapter has been an opportunity to review current parenting styles, assess your own style, and make adjustments if necessary. We learned that God has numerous character qualities, values and attributes that make Him perfect and wonderful. Although we can't be perfect, we can rely on our faultless and supreme God to help us with our children and teens. We also reminded ourselves that *Parenting with Power, Love and Sound Mind* is about raising children with loads of love and being consistent with discipline and tons of forgiveness. As we close this chapter, remember that God loves you and every member of your family. Through faith and reliance on Him, He will do a good work in you.

Questions for Reflection

1. Before reading this chapter, what was your view of God as a perfect parent? Were you right on track or did you need to adjust your thinking?
2. What are some of the characteristics of God that you can reflect on as you raise your children or teens?
3. Did you see yourself in any of the parenting styles listed above? If so, which ones and how will you go about making necessary changes?
4. How can you use the knowledge you've learned in this chapter to become a better parent?
5. What are some methods that you currently use as a parent which you are proud of and want to continue? What are some things you wish to modify?
6. Was the video game analogy helpful to you? How can you structure yourself to parent with a video game mentality?

Prayer for Today

Dear Father in Heaven, thank You for being a gracious, merciful, loving and powerful God. I so appreciate that You are a perfect parent who has my best interest and the interest of my family at heart. Thank You for helping me realize that I am not a perfect parent and that I do not have to become one, as that is impossible. I have You, Jesus and the Holy Spirit working and living in me to make me the best parent I can be. Help me to continue to see myself as You see me: as Your precious child with gifts, talents and abilities that You placed in me to do good works; an over-comer, a leader, the head and not the tail and more than a conqueror. I submit my life to You, Lord. I pray this in the Name of Jesus. Amen.

Chapter 3:
The Importance of Guarding Your Heart, Mind and Words

"A wise man's heart guides his mouth, and his lips promote instruction. Pleasant words are like a honeycomb, sweet to the soul and healing to the bone." (Proverbs 16:24)

This chapter is designed to teach you the importance of diligently safeguarding your heart (spirit) while consistently renewing your mind with positive, lovely, true and noble thoughts so that you can speak genuine words of love and kindness to your children and teens. We will first examine the root of hardened hearts, the infestation of negativity on the mind, and the lack of fruit-bearing words the condition produces. Then we'll talk about ways to make our hearts, minds and words bear good fruit and flourish. The chapter will conclude with a list of practical tools and techniques to help you increase communication and interaction with your children and teens.

I have counseled countless individuals who want to learn how to *Parent with Power, Love and Sound Mind.* What I have frequently found is that hardened hearts, negative thoughts and destructive words consistently interfere with victorious parenting. I met with a young mother and her teenage daughter. Even before the mother sat down on my couch it was obvious she was close to exploding. Before our first hellos, she began screaming about her other children at home, how bad they were, and how bitter, resentful and overwhelmed she was. She'd had so many negative experiences with her children that her heart had become hardened to them. Her mind told her that things would never get better and that her situation was hopeless. Her words were destructive and venomous.

As I glanced toward this woman's teenager, with tears flowing down her face, I instantly went into warrior mode. I decided that this mother and family were worth fighting for. They were wonderful people stuck in a pit of pessimism and were drowning in their circumstances. I shared all the things

I saw that were going right. Mom quieted and the teen slowly emerged from her shroud of sadness. By the end of the session, the duo was smiling, laughing and sharing all the strengths they saw in each another. They even came up with a plan on how to work together to create change in the house, with one another, and with the remaining children at home. The family is doing amazing and regularly sends me positivity-filled updates.

Guard Your Heart, Mind and Words

"Above all else, guard your heart for it is the wellspring of life. Put away perversity from your mouth; keep corrupt talk from your lips." (Proverbs 4:23-24)

The heart (spirit) is so integral to our very being that God specifically tells us to guard it. If we carefully choose what we allow into our hearts, we will be kept from walking down the wrong path and being held captive by our thoughts. Our speech to our children will be pure and clean.

Healthy, loving hearts are engorged with love, forgiveness, compassion and tenderness. Happy, content hearts filled with the fruits of the spirit produce health, life and joy to all who encounter them. Just as God commands us to guard our hearts, He also tells us to renew and keep our minds on higher, lovely things.

Protecting our hearts and controlling our thoughts is not easy. We need to constantly put in the work required to alter thinking that is not healthy or beneficial to our lives or the lives of the people around us. Every time an unhelpful thought comes to mind, it's important to cast it out and put our thinking back on track. When we use wisdom, discernment and judgment, and remove all foolishness from our thoughts, peace and self-control reign. What should thoughts contain? Philippians 4:4-8 gives us specific instructions about training our minds.

"Rejoice in the Lord always. I will say it again: Rejoice! Let your gentleness be evident to all. The Lord is near. Do not be anxious about anything but in everything, by prayer and petition, with thanksgiving, present your requests to God. And the peace of God, which transcends all understanding, will guard your hearts and your minds in Christ Jesus.

Finally brothers, whatever is true, whatever is noble, whatever is right, whatever is pure, whatever is lovely, whatever is admirable-if anything is excellent or praiseworthy-think about such things. Whatever you have learned or received or heard from me, or seen in me-put it into practice." (Philippians 4:4-8)

God tells us to praise Him, bring all of our cares to Him and be thankful. He wants us to meditate on thoughts that are splendid, righteous, prosperous and wholesome. Exile the rest!

How Hearts and Minds Get Polluted

Hearts and minds become hardened internally and externally. Internally, we experience hardened hearts and minds by living in unforgiveness, wrath, impurity, jealousy, rage, anger, selfishness, and strife.

When you have an argument with your spouse or child and don't settle it, when your boss refuses to give you the promotion you deserve and you feel a deep sense of anger, when church members are sharing testimony of blessing and abundance and you wonder, "Why not me?," when you ask your child to take care of something important and they forget, ignore you or say no.... all of these things, left to their own devices to simmer and soak into your core, will eventually cause your heart to harden and your mind to sink to low places. The consequences of a hardened heart and a defeated mind are tragic beyond description.

Externally, our hearts are hardened and our minds burdened by inappropriate use of television, radio, the Internet, billboard advertisements, magazines, newspapers and a constant barrage of violence, foul language, guns, drugs, alcohol and greed. All can produce a hardened heart, a negative mind, and a dark spirit.

Take a Stand, Make the Right Choice

"....But the fruit of the Spirit is love, joy, peace, patience, kindness, goodness, faithfulness, gentleness and self-control." (Galatians 5:16, 22-23)

It's important to choose which information you absorb. You can choose to forgive, to let God handle your current and future situations, and to feel blessed and highly favored for what you have. You can choose to see yourself and your child or teen as more than conquerors and leaders, as prosperous, victorious, healthy and carefree. You can choose to turn off the television, listen to Christian radio programs, search Christian websites, watch family friendly programs and put blocks on your computer. You can choose to avoid people who indulge in unwholesome activities. You can choose to live a healthy lifestyle.

Parenting with Power, Love and Sound Mind requires you to operate from a pure heart and mind. It requires you to see with the eyes of your loving heart, peaceful mind and from a winning position.

The Story of Joseph Carey Merrick, the Elephant Man
(August 5, 1862 — April 11, 1890)

"My life is full because I know I am loved." (Joseph Merrick)

Joseph Merrick lived in 18th-century England. Because of a congenital defect, Joseph was born grotesquely deformed. Before meeting the benevolent Dr. Frederick Treves, he was beaten, starved and paraded around regularly for people to gawk and poke fun. Joseph's head was so large that he had to place his back up against a wall when he slept, position his legs so his knees were near his midsection, and then place his head on his knees. Real rest was probably impossible for Mr. Merrick. It's believed that his deformities caused him to be in constant moderate to severe pain. To be forced to live in the manner Merrick lived would be isolating, frustrating and, to most of us, inconceivable. It would be entirely understandable if Mr. Merrick had a bad attitude or felt hopeless about his life. Instead, when asked about his life one day, Mr. Merrick said, "I am happy every minute of every hour of every day." (*The Elephant Man — A Study in Human Dignity,* Ashley Montagu, *1971 and lecture from Shawn Christopher Shea, M.D., April 2009 Syracuse, New York).*

For a man who suffered physically, emotionally and socially to feel as he did speaks volumes: You can control the softness of your heart and the thoughts that provide you with your personal view of the world. Joy and peace are an internal attitude. It is completely possible to have joy and peace, even while under extreme duress.

Mr. Merrick was described as having a kind, gentle and noble nature. He was also well known for his strong love and faith in God. Mr. Merrick believed God created him exactly the way he was supposed to be. It's my contention that Mr. Merrick's faith held him in constant peace. It also allowed him the contentment, happiness and joy that kept his thoughts pure and his heart warm. If Mr. Merrick had this kind of spirit within him, you can, too.

Why is renewing your mind, monitoring your thoughts and the story of Joseph Merrick important as you guide your children *with Power, Love and Sound Mind?* If you believe the best in yourself and in your child or teen you'll reach your goal: to speak Godly words of love and health to your offspring. Acting from a pure heart, battling every negative thought and forcing yourself into seeing from a positive, faith-filled perspective gives you a greater sense of peace, accomplishment and lightness. There is something sacred and calming about walking in integrity and self respect, with a light heart and a fresh mind. Living your life in this way allows you to draw your child or teen into doing the same.

The Power of Words

"A careless word may kindle strife; A cruel word may wreck a life, a bitter word may hate instill; A brutal word may smite and kill. A gracious word may smooth the way; A joyous word may light the day. A timely word may lessen stress; A loving word may heal and bless." (Author Unknown: from 30 Days to Taming the Tongue by Deborah Smith Pegues, 2005)

The Bible tells us that it's not what goes into the mouth but what comes out of it that defiles a man. (Matthew 15:11-20) As parents, our words to our children are powerful. *Parenting with Power, Love and Sound Mind* changes communication patterns so we empower rather than inadvertently cripple those we love. Just as we ought to fill our bellies with wholesome foods, we ought to fill our children's ears with nurturing concepts and nurturing communication.

Caution! Labeling Your Child Can Be Dangerous

As an adjunct professor of Short Term Intervention to Master's level students, the first speech my class hears is always the same: "We'll all work with individuals, young and old, who will come to us with diagnoses from A to Z. They'll be labeled Bi-Polar, Personality Disorder, Depression, Phobia, Anxiety, ADHD, Oppositional Defiant Disorder, and more. Work with the person, not the label, and tell the person up front that they are not their label."

I say this because I know the toxic power of labels and how they can "infect" a person with a vision of life or death. A person who identifies himself with the depression he's struggling with is a powerless victim, not a winning, victorious, overcomer. Placing mental health diagnoses on children breaks my heart; it sets them up to view themselves in that light and to adopt a negative mindset and portfolio, one with strict limitations. In addition, the child, his parents, and others may also begin to blame the behaviors on the label and to feel powerless about how to address the matter.

To *Parent with Power, Love and Sound Mind,* we must applaud and teach our children _while_ they're behaving because we want to foster good behavior so they'll repeat it and learn to honor it. Careless words damage young lives and cause pain. Watch your words and witness how your child or teen becomes a stellar role model for others.

Your Words Produce Results

"The tongue has the power of life and death and those who love it will eat its fruit." (Proverbs 18:21)

"Reckless words pierce like a sword, but the tongue of the wise brings healing." (Proverbs 12:18)

Just as God used words to create, He has given you the power of the spoken word to generate results in your life. As a parent, you have power and authority via the words you speak over your offspring.

James Chapter 3:1-12 tells how difficult, but necessary, it is to watch our words. If we don't, we can corrupt our entire body, family, and sphere of influence.

For such a small body part, the mouth has a tremendous influence. Fill your mouth with praise, love and devotion for your children at all times.

You can't afford to speak with mixed messages of blessing and cursing over your children. The messages of cursing can capture them and send them in the wrong direction.

"Do not let any unwholesome talk come out of your mouths, but only what is helpful for building others up according to their needs, that it may benefit those who listen......Get rid of all bitterness, rage and anger, brawling and slander, along with every form of malice. Be kind and compassionate to one another, forgiving each other, just as in Christ God forgave you." (Ephesians: 4:29-32)

A good friend shared a story about her sister and niece. My friend's niece suffers from terrible allergies and asthma, to the point that it keeps the girl from having a normal existence. She is regularly confined to a couch or her room because of her illness. She can't even go on a sleepover, every young girl's rite of passage, because she can't survive outside of her hypo-allergenic home.

As the girl would lie on her mother's lap, mom would stroke her head and confess over the child that she was sick, had allergies, and that they were destroying the child's life. Instead of speaking words of comfort and healing, she was speaking words of death.

As parents, you have authority over your children. You have authority over their wellbeing. Speaking negative words over your child will bring negative results.

If you tell your children they're not smart, they never listen, they always eat junk food and cannot sit still, they'll live out your prophecy. Likewise, if you tell your children they're righteous, specially gifted, articulate and thoughtful, they will feel it to their bones, and live out your prophecy! So before you speak to your children, remind yourself that words count and that they produce fruit, perfect or deformed, depending on how you use them. Bring into being the qualities and characteristics you want to see in your children by using the right words.

Miguel and Michelle

I met with a young mother, Michelle, and her son Miguel, age 8, as a favor to a friend of mine. He had called and said Miguel was frequently getting into trouble at school. The youngster had already been suspended several times and was almost impossible to control in class. He had a foul mouth and consistently put down the other children.

Miguel lacked the skills to engage in positive interaction and to show his greatness, gloriousness and godliness. It was all bottled up inside. Michelle, a struggling parent, had been feeding into his fury with verbal negativity almost from the day he was born. I was thrilled when Michelle agreed to meet with me to learn a new way of interacting with Miguel.

On our first meeting, Michelle brought Miguel along. When children attend a session, I make every effort to discourage all forms of negative communication. I know they're sitting with me because things aren't going well. I don't need the history. It's always my goal to move forward, not remain trapped in negativity.

But I met my match with Michelle. She was a beautiful woman with an intense personality and immense strength to match. No matter what I said, Michelle needed to tell me about their mental health disorders, all of the recent fights she had been in, and how many police reports had been written in the last few months for neighborhood altercations. Miguel contributed, too, because he had been in the audience for all of the shows. Michelle and Miguel would even get into debates over their differing views of how things "went down."

Finally, after much verbal wrestling, I was able to get Miguel and Michelle to quiet down and learn the principles and strategies I wanted to teach them. Michelle needed to be nurtured every bit as much as Miguel; they were two lonely ships together in a large sea of strangers. Her positivity bank was too empty to fill Miguel's, so negativity was spewing from every corner, crack and crevice.

My work with Miguel and Michelle took time. They eventually joined a neighborhood church and began to live in their God-given potential. As soon as Michelle saw the destructive nature of her mindset and behavior, she was able to change it. And when she changed her course, Miguel quickly followed suit.

God Will Help You

God doesn't leave you alone to make difficult changes without His help.

He is always available to you. God wants a relationship with you and wants praise, prayers, requests and worship to permeate your life as a parent. If you reach out to Him, He'll give you the desires of your heart and the words to use with your child or teen.

"The Lord said to him, "Who gave man his mouth? Who makes him deaf or mute? Who gives him sight or makes him blind? Is it not I, the Lord? Now go; I will help you speak and will teach you what to say."
(Exodus 4:11-12)

Moses, as leader of the nation of Israel, felt unsure of himself as the one who could lead the nation out of persecution and out of hiding. He saw himself as a father of a nation and wanted to care for those who depended on him, but he still struggled with insecurity. As a parent, you'll frequently find yourself feeling the same kind of uncertainty, but God is there for you every bit as intensely as He was there for Moses.

Helpful Strategies to Keep Your Heart, Words and Thoughts Pure

Spend Time in Scripture: I cannot stress enough how important it is for you to delve into Scripture. Your life depends on it. The more effort and time you spend reading God's Word, the clearer your focus, vision, and intentions will become. Your heart will be filled, your mind will be renewed, and your words will be overflowing with love. If you're not sure where to start, ask your pastor or a mature Christian friend. (2 Timothy 3: 16-17)

Pray: Talk to God. Ask Him how to be a parent. Learn His thoughts toward you and your family. (1 Thessalonians 5:16-18)

Praise God: Sing songs to and about God. Share with Him your daily adoration, worship and love. Tell Him how thankful you are that He is in your life, that you are a child of God, and that you are blessed and highly favored of the Lord. Give Him a complete and detailed description of what you're thankful for. (2 Samuel 22:50, Psalm 47:6, Psalm 147:1, 2 Corinthians 2:14)

Meditate: Christian meditation is a cleansing experience. To meditate effectively, quiet your body and mind. While meditating, listen with your spirit for the small, still voice of the Lord. Meditation is refreshing and revitalizing. I challenge you to meditate at least once a day. (Psalm 145:5)

Establish a Network of Godly People: Gather a support network around you that can provide you with Godly counsel and help you when you need it. Only put people into this network that you can trust to give you wise, truthful advice. Please note: It's important to have a social network of diverse individuals. Some should be in authority over you in the Lord; pastors, elders, deacons, ministry leaders or others who are highly trained in the Lord. Also include people who are equal to you in their walk with the Lord. These are the folks with whom you can share common interests and information. Finally, consider having a willing heart to mentor others with less knowledge in the Lord. All three types of people will keep you fresh and accountable, and will help you access a variety of expertise and knowledge. (Proverbs 15:22)

Practical Tools for Valuable Communication

Realize You Are Your Child's Favorite Toy. Has it ever occurred to you that, as a parent, you are your child's favorite toy? Although it may sound silly at first, think about it for a minute. Children love to be amused and to know they're the center of the universe.

My family and I just returned home from a lovely night out to dinner. A table of couples sitting next to us were talking loudly and having a great time swapping stories about themselves and their children. One man told the party that he thoroughly enjoyed being the baby of the house for six years before his sister came along. He related that the one thing he loved about being the baby is that "a thousand adults doted on me and my every whim at all times."

This story made me think of the "Toy Store" analogy. Children really do see their parents as their "favorite toys." Parents have more features, actions, reactions, moods and displays of human emotion than any other toy or game in their toy boxes.

How do children behave when they get a new toy? They check out every aspect of it. My son, Chandler, is a car fanatic. He has hordes of cars, trucks and other machines in his collection. Every time Chandler gets a new vehicle he becomes enthralled. He makes sure the mini doors and hood open, that the paint color is just right and of course, the tires and rims must be up to snuff. When he finds a vehicle that is jam-packed with features he loves, he comes back to it time after time. If my son receives a vehicle that is not up to his expert standards, he just puts it aside and it's never looked at again.

Your children are like this with you. They're masters at figuring you out and engaging with you in a way that promises your full attention. They know how to "push your buttons" to get you animated and emotional. You may turn red, the veins may pop out of your neck, your voice may sound like you are on a megaphone and you can sure come up with a lot of words to describe how you're feeling.

The "well-behaved" or "compliant" child may not conclude that you are more interesting when things are going wrong, but for the challenging and intense child, it's quite likely that you're viewed as being much more responsive and available when things are off beam, and that you are boring and disengaged when things are going well. Relying on this acute, but immature, sense of observation, a difficult child will realize he gains more attention from you by acting in ways that displease you. Your child has not made a decision to act out in defiance, but is doing what he's doing based on results: his toy lights up when he behaves in certain ways. Somewhere within his little mind, he has learned to attract your attention by misbehaving. Become the parent whose bells, whistles, sounds and lights go off when your child is doing all the right things.

Master Good Non-Verbal Communication: Sixty-six percent of human communication is non-verbal. When speaking to your child, think about how you look to them. Use good eye contact; go to their eye level. If they're small, bend down and speak with them. Make sure your face is neutral when imposing consequences, and fill it with limitless smiles and happiness when you share your child's successes. Watch your posture; keep your body open (arms should not be folded or on your hips). Stay at a comfortable distance to show respect for your child's natural boundary for personal space. Be affectionate, smile, hug, shake hands, tap knuckles, pat them on the back, wink, and use other common physical expressions of care and concern.

Listen: Convey a general attitude that expresses abundant, genuine curiosity toward your child. Don't speak, judge, interrupt or have preconceived notions about where the conversation is going. Instead, empty your mind. Stay in a constant state of delight with a desire to be informed. Accept their point of view and commend them for having a spirit of individuality. (James 1:19, Proverbs 18:13)

Timing: Remember too, that children get tired, have bad days, get hungry, fall ill and get upset, just as we do. Before starting a conversation, make sure none of these things will have an effect on the outcome.

Ask Open-Ended Questions: An open-ended question requires more than a yes or no answer. It asks your child to think and share information. When you ask open-ended questions, you'll learn how your child sees the world. The more open-ended questions you ask, and genuinely listen to, the more you'll get to know your child's heart. Good open-ended questions promote growth and learning while promoting a two-way discussion and building relationship.

Here are a few examples of open-ended questions:

"Tasha, what kind of things do you think about when you have to make a big decision?" "After you make a decision, what lets you know that it was the right one?" "What does it feel like inside?"

"Nicholas, what are some things that make you super-happy?" "How do you know they make you happy?" "What does happy feel like inside?"

Open-ended questions reveal the condition of your child's heart, their portfolio, their thinking and the words they use. They provoke deeper thought and produce wisdom, knowledge and discernment.

Of course, the examples above are best used with older children and teens. Modify your questions to the age of your child. For a four-year-old, an open-ended question might be, "What is your favorite color?" "Where can I find that color?" Engage with your kids while everyone is calm and enjoying each other's company, or when your child is seeking advice from you. Try to ask questions that give children the ability to learn the answers on their own.

A great place to have powerful conversations with children is in the car because they're trapped. When your child responds, encourage more dialogue by being empathetic and respectful. Don't give the impression that you're going to threaten, criticize, put-down, judge, accuse or be sarcastic. If you're unclear about what your child is saying, politely ask for more explanation.

Have a Sense of Humor: Laughter truly is the best medicine. It reduces stress and fends off illness. It distracts attention, reduces tension, changes expectations and increases endorphins. Humor establishes and fosters warm interpersonal relationships. It's a great way to release anger, hostility and aggression.

Laughter can help a child manage shame or embarrassment and help lift depression. When using humor, be sure it can be understood by the child, shared with other people, and that it's harmless. Humor is a tool that lightens the burdens of life. Laugh often with your children, and with yourself.

I recently attended a seminar on laughter. The presenter told us the average adult laughs just 4 times a day; while the average child laughs 146 times per day, so this is an area where we could be learning from our children! Be an adult who laughs and expresses the joy in your heart. (Psalm 126:2)

Create Quality Time: Creating quality time is essential to communication and interaction with your children. Be present in your child's life and ensure that the time you spend together will develop your child's sensibilities and preferences. In a therapy session with a young man whose mother had passed away two years previously, I could see that the fellow's spirit was broken because he was trying to remember times that just the two of them had been alone together. Out of the fourteen years of his life, he could only come up with two times that being alone with his mother had happened. Allow his sad experience to be a wake up call for your family. Quality time with a parent is essential. It's imperative to slow yourself down from the hustle and bustle of life and designate special time for just you and your child.

I had the opportunity to take Savannah to a mother-daughter retreat. What a lovely time! We were able to pray together, create a commemorative art piece to remember the event, and establish a creed for our relationship. My daughter still talks about the event and how much it blessed her life. We've decided to make it an annual event. If you don't have time to go to a special retreat, don't worry. Your child will be content with a walk, a trip to the ice cream store, or a board game. A child's expectations are simple: they just want to be with you and vigorously soak in all of your love for them. It isn't rocket science, I promise!

All of the above-named basic communication skills will help you advance in every area of your life. They provide you with the tools you need to build a solid relationship with your child (or anyone else, for that matter). When used correctly, their wisdom and methodologies will infuse into your child's spirit and soul. Behaving in this manner allows your child to see you as a positive role model and helps them to learn and adopt the skills themselves. These skills, along with the techniques in following chapters, will inspire your child to become magnificent in every way possible.

Provide Firsthand Experiences: Part of the battle plan of success is to provide your child with firsthand experiences as opposed to secondhand ones. Secondhand experiences come in the form of books, movies and lectures. With secondhand experiences, your children learn from watching rather than experiencing or doing. Secondhand methods tend to have less impact. And secondhand experiences can backfire because a child is left to his own devices to internalize what he is seeing and he can make mistakes in interpretation. Firsthand experiences are optimal because you literally share with the child all the things you see that are going right while they are happening.

Under Parenting *with Power, Love and Sound Mind* you'll take firsthand experiences and infuse them with descriptive positive dialogue, with verbal and non-verbal communication about what's going right rather than what's going wrong. This strategy allows your child to internalize and own the positive, honorable characteristics he's displaying and allows him to feel a sense of accomplishment and healthy pride. Capture and give your power to only positive moments; let your child know he is becoming greater and greater at every turn. Remember to stay in the now and show pleasure for things that are happening in the moment, regardless of the past or future behaviors or challenges that may occur. (James 1:22)

Be truthful, genuine and filled with love in every circumstance: Always use the truth of the moment and share it with your child. Even when you're asked to create success for a child who is seemingly struggling to find success, be honest and patient. Being truthful takes away your child's ability to refute the goodness you're establishing as belonging to him.

Everlasting Change Will Occur

As you master the approach, the above techniques and life philosophy, your child will begin to renovate his current portfolio and put a new positivity-filled portfolio into action. The more successes a child can claim, the more data he can retrieve from within when he's going through trials and conflicts. Your child will become skilled at navigating challenges with great achievement and will live in a righteous, fruit-filled way. As inner wealth, inner strength, greatness and godliness develops, your child will stop being affected by peer pressure and will instead pick friends with higher standards and loftier goals. Your child will treat his body well, avoid high-risk behaviors, become more obedient, and find more joy in life. Your child will begin to pursue a life of integrity that is purpose-driven.

You'll see your child obtain mastery over his intensity and channel it in healthier and more positive ways. Most importantly, the change will be permanent because it will occur from the inside out. Your child will see himself as valued and loved, and he'll share with the world from that portfolio. Every success will give him a deeper understanding of his ability to achieve great things.

Chapter Summary

Through His Word, God has commanded us to guard our hearts, take captive our thought-life and watch our words. It's hard work to do all of that — but it can be done. Declare the Word of God over yourself and your children; believe with all of your heart that the Word will manifest itself in your life. Keep a positive perspective, diligently watch what goes into your mind from external sources, and speak from a position of love at all times. Spend time in scripture, prayer, praise and meditation. Create a diverse support system of individuals. Know that you are your child's favorite toy. Master good non-verbal communication; listen with all of your power from a position of genuine curiosity. Be mindful of timing, ask open-ended questions to engage your child, and learn who they are on the inside. Have a sense of humor, spend quality time with them, provide them with first hand experiences and always be truthful.

Questions for Reflection

1. Reflect on the condition of your heart. Do you need heart surgery, a little diet and exercise to improve its health, or are you in tip-top shape?
2. What are your thoughts? Do you need to take your thoughts captive and transform them to a more Godly vision of your life?
3. How are your words? In what areas do you need improvement?
4. Who are the people in your support system? Do all of them provide comfort and sound counsel?
5. Take a look at all of the above practical techniques. Going one by one write, quietly reflect or discuss ways in which you already use these methods and how you can advance in them further.
6. Make an effort to look around the world in which you live and soak in all the beauty around you. If you find that you default to the negative, do what you've learned and are learning: switch your default to positive. Look for the strengths in people and the joy of nature.

Prayer for Today

Lord, help me to have a pure heart and a pure mind filled with love and adoration for You. Help me keep the thoughts of my head and the meditations of my heart on You and Your Word. Help me to use wisdom, knowledge, understanding and discernment when I speak to my child. May my words be seasoned with grace and love, and only be used for their benefit, the way You would raise them. May the words of my mouth be pleasing to You. I pray these things in Your Holy Name, my Rock, my Lord, my Jesus! Amen!

TRANSFORMING THE WAY YOU VIEW AND INTERACT WITH YOUR CHILD OR TEEN

This section of *Parenting with Power, Love and Sound Mind* will help you gain a different perspective about your child. Howard Glasser began using the term portfolios while working with challenging children and teens to help parents get a firm picture in their minds about what happens internally during every interaction. The following pages will show you how to begin purposefully and creatively inspiring a portfolio filled with positivity within your child and turn your challenging child's behavior from overwhelming to overcoming and victorious.

Chapter 4:
Developing Positive Portfolios:
The Law of Reaping
and Sowing

In this chapter, we discuss loving our intense children unconditionally, just as they are. We will discuss the need and ways to create a positive "portfolio" for our children and to use the law of reaping and sowing to our advantage. As parents, we can create success, victory and triumph in our children's lives. We will revisit the need to watch our words, to live with an encouraging, upbeat perspective and to use proper agendas and intentions to create overflowing portfolios of sensational success.

Circus Dreams

To experience an intense person's "playground," there's nothing better than a superb, upscale circus show. My family and I went to a popular acrobatic circus. My daughter, Savannah, was so mesmerized that she forgot to breathe or to keep her jaw closed. She was paralyzed by her excitement, perched on the edge of her seat. As mentioned earlier, Savannah is an intense person. She's in motion most of the time and enjoys it thoroughly. So what brought Savannah to a point of comatose behavior?

Seeing people like herself in action. Without exaggerating, I think this colorful and activity-filled circus is my daughter's ideal vision of heaven.

If you're not familiar with an upscale acrobatic circus, they are wonders to the senses. The performers — skilled acrobats, jugglers, dancers, singers, gymnasts and contortionists — come from all over the world. Wearing lively colors, they flip, fly and jump through the air above a brilliant decorated stage. Many things are happening at once. It is an auditory and visual experience that is both captivating in the moment and completely unforgettable afterward.

I, too watched, mesmerized, as performers from diverse backgrounds and cultures shared their special abilities — contorting their bodies to become frogs, snakes, monkeys and trees, balancing on cans while rocking on a board, positioning their torsos and limbs in body-bending, mind-blowing ways, jumping rope as a group with multiple ropes, and soaring through the air in butterfly costumes. These are intense people and it is glorious to observe.

Intensity Is a Gift

"I'm a very intense person. When I go after something, I want to go after it with everything I have. I want to push myself to the edge."
(Greg Norman: professional golfer)

Intensity is in every child to some degree. It's a God-given trait. It is intensity, inner wealth, inner strength, godliness, gloriousness, vision, faith and reliance on God that determines someone's success in life. Apathetic individuals rarely get far; they fail to recognize and "own" their intrinsic potential and worth. It's the intense dreamers and doers — filled with passion and energy — that make the world a fun and fascinating place to be. When children and teens are taught to embrace their intensity and allowed space for it to soar, they become skilled at taking control and using it appropriately.

"For you created my inmost being; you knit me together in my mother's womb, I praise you because I am fearfully and wonderfully made; your works are wonderful, I know that full well. My frame was not hidden from you when I was made in the secret place. When I was woven together in the depths of the earth, your eyes saw my unformed body. All the days ordained for me were written in your book before one of them came to be."
(Psalm 139:13-16)

The psalmist David clearly states that God knew each of us even before He made us. This means He created your child to be intense. He has a plan for all of that power, force and concentration. He knew what He was doing when He gave your child to you and nobody else. He was confident you would know how to channel all of that strength and might in the right direction. When you feel like this job is too much, remind yourself of your own God-given gifts and that God doesn't give you more than you can handle. So when you know, to the core of your being, that you're *not* measuring up, remember this:

When you're at the end of your rope, take a breath, step back, and give *yourself* a brief, uncritical reset! It works wonders!

"Consider it pure joy, my brothers, whenever you face trials of many kinds, because you know that the testing of your faith develops perseverance. Perseverance must finish its work so that you may be mature and complete, not lacking anything. If any of you lacks wisdom, he should ask God, who gives generously to all without finding fault, and it will be given to him." (James 1:2-5)

At times God will have a particular way of giving you gifts (including children) that stretch and develop you. He knows you're tenacious and that you'll advocate for an intense child with enough personal power and integrity to do whatever it takes to help him or her succeed in life. As a parent, you know your children's needs and your own limits, and you know when to reach out to God and to the people He places in your life to help you. When you reach out to God, he will give you wisdom and comfort.

The Typical View of Intensity

To review, intensity is defined as exceptionally great concentration, power, or force. Intensity is in everyone to some degree. All children can be intense at times, but some are intense more often than what you may consider the norm. Children can be physically intense (in constant movement) or emotionally/mentally intense (sitting or talking for hours working on a project that thrills and fascinates them, or deep in thought).

Unfortunately, most folks view intensity, particularly in children, as something to be modified or squashed. I think this is because intense children don't conform to traditional norms. Livewires require authority figures to "think outside the box" and tap into new ways of learning, teaching, doing and being. When children and teens get negative feedback about their intensity, they begin to feel they're "wired wrong" in some way, that they are somehow intrinsically "bad." Intense children and teens are at times described, or experienced as, overbearing, too fast, too loud or excitable, annoying, hyper, non-compliant, socially behind the curve, difficult, crazy, jumpy, oppositional, inattentive, unfocused, and so on. How do any of these labels help a child or a teen develop inner wealth, a sense of mission, or a strategy that can enable him or her to move mountains? What we indicate to children about their way of being in the world, whether spoken or unspoken, can be as crippling as tying both arms behind their backs, blindfolding them, and then saying, "Go out and make it happen! I believe in you (except for your …)!"

Not long ago, I was chatting with a teacher about her elementary students. At first, she told me that her classroom was filled with positivity and elation, except for "one boy" she just couldn't get a handle on. She was annoyed by the little boy because she couldn't control his behavior and didn't think he could, either. She said, "He walks around when he isn't supposed to, sways and bothers other children during floor time, and speaks out of turn during share time."

To my horror, she said she sighed with relief when his mother *finally* took him to the doctor and got medication to control his behavior. She was relieved because the boy was now, to her way of thinking),"under control." And because his intense behaviors lessened, my teacher friend could once again teach in peace. She had her happy ending but I was nearly apoplectic!

As much as I love my friend and respect her gift of teaching, she is wrong about accepting medication as a first, rather than a last, step to control this boy. In fact, she unwittingly **encouraged** his prior actions by stopping the proceedings in class to acknowledge his inappropriate behaviors at every turn. She would ignore him whenever he was behaving, so to his mind, he became invisible (lacking any real relationship) whenever he behaved!

This boy had learned **the wrong lessons** from his classroom, his teacher, his parents and his pediatrician:
- to be noticed, I need to disobey;
- the medicine makes me a more acceptable person;
- I can't control myself, and no one else can control me, without the medicine;
- When I do obey and am deemed "acceptable," I become invisible and everyone seems happier;
- I guess there's something very wrong about wanting to be in the thick of things and engaging, so I won't do that anymore so everyone around me will be happier.

Depression, suicide, apathy, aggression and anger are all symptomatic of people who have much to give and the intensity and energy to give it, but have been "shut down."

The Truth about Intensity

As mentioned earlier, intensity in children and adults is a special gift from God. Medicating to counteract intensity is foolish, not to mention dangerous to a child's sense of inner wealth; it reduces their power and puts it out of reach. Intensity, when channeled in the right direction, can be used in a positive way.

Jesus was an intense child: purpose-driven, goal-oriented, with an intense interest in fulfilling the Father's will for his life. Should his parents have spent more time controlling him? After all, he stayed behind in the Jerusalem temple and it took them three days to find him again! (Luke 2:41-50) As a mother myself, I have no doubt that Mary was freaking out by day three!

Biblical figureheads like Abraham, Moses, John the Baptist, Mary, Ruth, David and Paul—to name just a few—all were intense. They were passionate, creative and dedicated to their cause and purpose; they all went against the norm of their time to reach their God-given vision for their lives. Thank God their parents loved and embraced them as they were!

Intensity Can Be Found Everywhere Today

Intensity is everywhere you look: athletes, musicians, singers, scientists on the brink of a major breakthrough, chefs looking to perfect taste and presentation, firefighters, police officers, symphony conductors, inventors, accountants looking to balance the books to the penny, artists, farmers who work day and night in every kind of weather, pastors, CEOs of companies. Intense people are perfecting their crafts everywhere you look. Intensity is not only okay—it is VITAL, and a very special gift from God.

Think of the songs we sing to our young children about being themselves, about letting their talents shine through. Do we really mean it? When your child is being uniquely himself and inadvertently draws attention to himself or to you as his parent, how does it make you feel? I hope, for your child's sake, that it makes you feel just fine. Here is one of those songs:

This Little Light of Mine: Version 2
Written By: Unknown, Copyright: Unknown
"This little light of mine,
I'm gonna let it shine
This little light of mine,
I'm gonna let it shine
This little light of mine,
I'm gonna let it shine
Let it shine,
Let it shine,
Let it shine.

Hide it under a bushel? No!
I'm gonna let it shine
Hide it under a bushel? No!
I'm gonna let it shine
Hide it under a bushel? No!
I'm gonna let it shine
Let it shine,
Let it shine,
Let it shine...........

The You-Tube Boy and His Auntie

A colleague arrived around Christmastime one year with a huge smile, excited to show off her nephew, a kindergartner. He was in his first Christmas play. She glowed with pride as she shared the video she would soon be posting on You Tube.

The video showed a quiet, angelic scene of baby Jesus lying in the manger. Mary, Joseph, the wise men and all the farm animals were staring at the new born babe and quietly singing "Silent Night." During the song, one of the wise men stepped out of formation. My colleague's nephew played air guitar in an intense, animated way and screamed (as opposed to singing) the lyrics to "Silent Night" at the top of his lungs while he danced, swirled, moon-walked and shimmied back and forth near the manger. It was obvious he was having a·blast; Auntie couldn't have felt more blessed. She saw in her nephew a desire to be different, an enthusiasm for God, and a way to express himself without fear of ridicule.

The little rocker's parents, on the other hand, were allegedly in their seats, cowering in embarrassment, hoping the song would end soon. What would people think? Their son had just "ruined" the play.

On the contrary: their son did not ruin the play. Everyone laughed for days about his animated, energetic theatrical debut. And the other cast members? All displayed great focus and responsibility as they kept the correct pace and tone with the song and stayed in their designated spots. All was well in the manger.

After my colleague finished sharing the video and story with me, my parting words were: "Well done, Auntie! You are a person who sees with visionary eyes and who embraces differences and life with zest."

Take Your Child's Intensity and Run with it!

If you have an intense child, foster her power. Take her drive and channel it in the direction it needs to go. When you do, she'll be the fruit-bearing success story you know in your heart she's destined to be. As a parent, it's your job to learn your child's skills, talents, abilities and gifts. When you do, you can guide her in the right direction. This will bless you, bless your child, and bless the world we all live in.

Remember— *especially on days when you feel like screaming* — that intensity is a gift and God wants you to help your child turn that gift into something that benefits His Kingdom. He gave an intense child to you because He knew you could handle it and would be obedient in fostering it and channeling it appropriately, to the glory of God.

Now let's take a look at a way you can help your child harness his inner wealth and inner strength so it can be used by God.

What's in Your Child's Portfolio?

Part of the work you will do to help your intense child or teen is to check into his current "portfolio." A personal portfolio is the list of words and beliefs your child uses to describe himself based on what he has heard and learned from the people and world around him.

It's easy to spot a child with a negative portfolio. He feels he's ugly, unlovable, helpless, hopeless, and friendless. He is depressed. By contrast, a child with a positive portfolio sees himself as likeable, lovable, strong, talented, good at making decisions, and well able to tackle problems.

When children with negative portfolios are asked to come up with three strengths or qualities that are good about them, they tend to have a difficult time with the answer. They truly don't know. In sharp contrast, if you ask the same child what it is about them that people don't like, they can rattle off a long list. Ask the same question to someone with a positive portfolio, and he'll be able to list his desirable traits rather quickly.

You can check your child's portfolio by reviewing what your child has been hearing from you and others. Clean out any areas that are not godlike, and fill them instead with positivity and helpful character qualities.

How We Develop Portfolios of Who We Are

"A cheerful heart is good medicine, but a crushed spirit dries up the bones." (Proverbs 17:22)

Portfolios begin at birth. We develop our portfolios each time we accept what others say about us. And what we accept is what we begin to believe about ourselves. If our children consistently hear from us or from others, "Stop that!" "Don't," "Sit Down," "I told you not to touch that," "How come you always squirm so much?" "You are so stupid," and other similar comments, they adopt (internalize) the negative information. Even if these words were spoken with the best of intentions, a child internalizes them as personal failure. Just imagine hearing any of the above statements about yourself, even now as an adult with the speaking and thinking skills to debate and deny what is being said. What a child hears is, "I'm a failure or a disappointment in so many ways."

A portfolio is filled in a positive way when people say things that enlighten and inform and are filled with love and genuine truth. "I see you sitting there quietly playing your game. You're concentrating, relaxing and peaceful. Thank you for managing your intense emotions so well." "I know you wanted to go on this play date, and it's hard to hear that your friend had to change his plans. You're behaving very powerfully right now. I am so proud of you!" "You're eating at the table and using good manners. You could be throwing your food, chewing with your mouth open and rocking in your chair. You're not breaking the rules, and instead are choosing to use good self-control."

Do you hear all of the values and good characteristics that are being taught in those few sentences? The sentences make a child feel good to be noticed. When you share what is going well and the characteristics that are being displayed, children are filled with internalized success.

It's vital to make sure your children are having their portfolios filled with love and acceptance for who they are. Acknowledge what each is doing well, what is happening that is right and what is not happening that would make things pleasant. For example, "You're not hitting or screaming right now". When you hold an intention for your child, the words you're using with him MUST match. In this way, his portfolio will change to one filled with positivity, inner wealth, inner strength, godliness, gloriousness and greatness.

The Law of Reaping and Sowing

Your child's portfolio is based on the biblical concept of reaping and sowing.

"A man reaps what he sows... the one who sows to please the Spirit, from the Spirit will reap eternal life. Let us not become weary in doing good for at the proper time we will reap a harvest if we do not give up. Therefore, as we have opportunity, let us do good to all people, especially to those who belong to the family of believers."
(Galatians 6:7-10)

Your words develop your child spiritually, mentally and physically. If your words are negative, your child will reap what you sow. If your words are positive, your child's positive portfolio will grow.

A child brought up with words that keep score of her inappropriate behavior learns to see herself as "bad" or "wrong." The negative connotations outweigh and eventually bankrupt any positive expressions of worthiness or honor. To create a successful portfolio, simply "flip-flop;" spend more effort, time and discussion with your child when things are going well, and offer a simple, very brief "reset" or time-out when things are going badly. Then get back to validating the wisdom your child shows in complying with the reset and setting things right again.

I've worked with hundreds of children and teenagers. The ones who are making poor choices and getting in the most trouble are packed with pessimistic, unenthusiastic views of themselves. Troy, a sixteen-year-old who found himself bored one night, broke into a string of neighbors' homes and was subsequently caught. While sitting in my office, I asked him what he thought of himself. His reply was that he was a "piece of garbage" that would end up in jail one day. He went on to say that his parents, his uncle and a couple of his teachers had told him that for years.

Troy did go on to spend time in jail for his actions. But he continued seeing me, and I shared with him the strengths I saw in him: "Troy, you're a good communicator and an excellent confidant who cares deeply about the safety and well-being of your friends. You're someone who truly wants to be enthusiastic and make a constructive impact on the world."

Troy heard me, but it took many sessions to get him to believe that I meant what I was saying and that I truly believed in his ability to re-channel his energies. I had to give him numerous and constant truthful examples to back up my claims of the greatness within him. Troy was so used to referring to the miserable, problem-oriented portfolio that was instilled in him, he had a difficult time buying truth from any other perspective.

Hannah, an eighteen-year-old, grew up in a house overflowing with love and care. From birth, she heard she was a gift of God, with talents and character galore. Her parents shared all the wonderful things they saw in her, and accentuated all of Hannah's affirmative character traits. Hannah went on to graduate from her class with top honors and a full scholarship to a prestigious private college. She was not "spoiled" or "cocky." Hannah was one of the biggest volunteers in her school and community. If there was a cause, she signed up to help; she saw herself as needed and valuable. Her vision and desires lay outside herself.

"Let us not become weary in doing good for at the proper time we will reap a harvest if we do not give up." (Galatians 6:9)

It is essential that our intention be to reap good fruit when we sow good fruit into our children. To do this, we must sow into our children nutritionally valuable, delicious words that are truthful and genuine. God knows this isn't always easy; that's why in the above passage, He tells us to not give up or get weary in doing good. Rely on Him, and He will help you stay focused on the right words to bring forth fruit. I'm confident, since you're reading this book, that you're the kind of parent who can and will sow seeds of blessing for your child.

> *"Whoever sows generously will also reap generously."*
> *(2 Corinthians 9:6)*

Remember! The more you strengthen a behavior, the more it will be repeated and the more it will become a part of who your child is. If you don't like a specific behavior, don't give energy to it. Provide delicious, descriptive language only at times when commendable behavior is occurring; provide a quick, simple "reset" when things are heading south.

When a child begins to get more comfortable receiving information for successes, he'll internalize the feeling of accomplishment. He will also learn to notice your response to those successes. This will cause him to hunt for success like a heat-seeking missile on its way to a target.

The Toll Taker: Keeping a Positive Perspective

"Two men looked out from prison bars; one saw mud, the other saw stars."
(Frederick Langbridge)

Everything we do in life is based on how we choose to see things and how we internalize what we encounter. No matter what happens, you get to choose how you view life. Your outlook is in your control and should be used wisely (as you already learned in the previous chapters). **Create success by choosing to see success in every moment.**

I have heard Howard Glasser tell the "Toll Taker" story and others have given an account of it a number of different ways. This is my interpretation of how it goes:

There once was a man who was studying dance at a local college. While going to school, he worked at the San Francisco toll bridge. Another man was waiting to pull up to a booth to pay and noticed the attendant dancing, smiling and having a genuinely good time. When the driver reached the toll booth, he asked the attendant why he was so happy. The attendant responded, "This is the best job in the world. I get to practice my dance moves, sing, and I have the best view of the Bay, the Bridge and of the City." The driver, impressed with the attendant, then asked about his much-less-animated co-workers. The attendant replied, "You mean those guys in the stand up coffins? They're no fun!"

The toll booth story is all about perspective. How important it is! Having a hope and faith-filled perspective is vital to living a Christian life.

When a parent walks into a teenager's room they can choose to see the clothes on the floor, the dressers strewn with adolescent treasures and a bed half made (if at all). Or they can walk into the room and see their teenager's personality, the one jacket hung up, the posters neatly tacked to the wall. It's all a matter of perspective. Keep your eyes on the prize and choose to see your child's strengths and efforts. When you are having difficulty locating and communicating strengths to your child, follow the example of Shamu's trainers.

Shamu: How to Create Success in Children Where None Seems to Exist

Have you ever wondered how Sea World trainers encourage a gigantic marine mammal to jump to higher heights than he would have in his natural surroundings? Here's the secret: the trainers started by placing a rope at the bottom of the tank and showering Shamu with praise, stroking, and feeding every time he swam over the rope.

At first, Shamu was granted success for just doing something that was literally unavoidable! The giant orca was just being and doing what came naturally. With each "success," the trainer raised the rope a little higher and continued rewarding Shamu every time he went over the rope. If he went under the rope, he received no interaction, no fish, no stroking, no reward. By encouraging his success and ignoring the whale's failures in this way, eventually Shamu learned to jump more than 20 feet into the air. *The trainer established an environment of success; there was absolutely no other option. Shamu was essentially elevated into success by providing him with high levels of affirmation every time he swam and jumped over the rope.*

At times intense children are so awash in negative life force that we need to prominently place them into positions of success by creating the accomplishment for them. For many, waiting to "catch" your child doing something successful could take weeks if not longer, so in those circumstances we have to be more resourceful. We need to start small and aim high while creating success.

As soon as a child experiences triumph and internalizes it as a welcome feeling, he'll begin to enjoy it and want more of it. He will begin to actually seek success and then will integrate it into his life.

Trevor

I had a chance to "Shamu" a young man named Trevor. Trevor had a reputation for being a "troublemaker," and for being someone who "was going nowhere." Trevor's portfolio was crammed with pessimism and misery. When Trevor got kicked out of class, he was sent to me to "be fixed."

Trevor came to my door, hair covering his eyes, hoodie pulled tightly around his face, in an obvious state of irritation. As he slumped in his chair, I introduced myself, welcomed him and let him know how pleased I was with him.

Trevor moved the hair out of his eyes just enough so he could see "the crazy lady" who was talking to him. You see, Trevor was expecting me to be like everyone else. I was supposed to follow the plan of all my predecessors and begin laying into Trevor for all of his misdeeds.

Instead, I told him how delighted I was that he didn't throw any chairs, swear, or harm anyone as he left the class he was told to leave. I let him know that those behaviors were entirely available to him, and that instead he had chosen to demonstrate self-control even under the pressure of intense frustration. I told him that his more measured response to the situation showed great use of personal power. I also noted that he could follow rules because he obeyed the teacher when asked to leave, showing grand qualities of strength and greatness.

By the time I finished listing all of the fabulous skills Trevor had demonstrated just in getting himself to my office, his hoodie was off, he was sitting at attention and was pushing his bangs back with his hand.

Trevor and I went on to have a marvelous and therapeutic relationship. He has never again been kicked out of a classroom. He has joined a vocational program and is well on his way to a fine career in a field he loves.

Taking a bleak situation and turning it into a success by choosing to accentuate the things that go right, works and it's the proper, Godly way to honor another person. Just a few sentences allowed me to establish a relationship and begin the transformation in Trevor's portfolio.

Parenting with Proper Agendas and Intentions Creates Prospering Portfolios

"For I know the plans I have for you" declares the Lord, "plans to prosper you and not harm you, plans to give you hope and a future."
(Jeremiah 29:11)

Creating a sound portfolio and working from a perspective of reaping and sowing requires you to set proper agendas and intentions for your child. The intentions you hold for them shows that you have high expectations and believe the best for them.

An agenda is simply a list of some things that he must do. Positive agendas uphold correct intentions. Negative agendas destroy the intentions you are trying to create.

An intention is a deliberate and purposeful long-term desire. It requires a plan or goal.

Every choice you make and every action you take creates a consequence — good or bad — in life. When you think in the short term, you work with an agenda. Intention and vision keep you enjoying the present moment but with a confidence that the future will be meaningful and blessed. For example, if you see your child doing something displeasing, you could choose to yell or scowl at him and give him the silent treatment for an hour so he knows you're upset. But if your intention is to teach him how to handle strong emotions and to forgive, you'll think twice about taking that course of action. Your option of screaming and stewing doesn't fit the intention or vision you've dedicated to teaching your child.

Zechariah and Elizabeth were parents who parented with intention for their son, John the Baptist. (Luke 1:57-80) They held fast and strong to the name bestowed on John even when peer pressure was upon them.

What it Means to Live with Intention for Your Child

"Now faith is being sure of what we hope for and certain of what we do not see." (Hebrews 11:1)

Visualize how you want your child to behave and how you want her to live, in character and deed. Keep your visualization in mind, even when your child displays evidence which is contrary to it.

Your intention must be positive and based on the qualities of character that you want your child to develop. If you want your child to have good table manners, firmly place into your mind a clear picture of your intention, then share your picture with your child in descriptive, success-based language to get her moving toward your intention.

Intentions to Hold for Your Child

Here are a few suggestions about character content that are wise intentions to hold for your child: perseverance, compassion, sharing, gentleness, a loving heart, peacefulness, patience, kindness, selflessness. Visualize what your child will look like while displaying each characteristic and don't let go of it.

For example, my good friend and colleague, Katherine Teasdale Edwards, was struggling to get her oldest daughter, Holly, off to school. Holly was not yet comfortable with separating from her parents, so going to school was traumatic for everyone involved. At first, the parents' agenda was to get Holly to stop clinging and crying every day before school. Then they realized they were acting out of an unhelpful agenda rather than out of intention.

What Katherine and her husband really wanted to instill in Holly was a feeling of fearlessness and comfort when she was in new settings so she could feel good about it. As soon as they switched from agenda to intention, their anger and frustration — mixed with sadness and depression about having to leave their poor sad child at school — diminished. They began visualizing Holly going to school without any drama and connected all the dots that would allow her to do so. And even before Holly managed the transition, her parents believed she could do it without a scene. They kept that picture in mind every morning, which de-escalated their own emotions. Slowly but surely, they put on happy faces every school morning and had Holly say as she walked up the school steps, "I am brave, I am smart and I can do it." Every day going to school became a bit easier for Holly until eventually it became no big deal. I'm happy to report that Holly is now gleefully going to school. She is a healthy, beautiful child filled with inner wealth and joy. Her parents are Nurtured Heart Christian parents who want the best for their family and the world around them.

Examples of specific intentions to hold for your child are: My daughter is GREAT because God created her exactly the way He wanted her; God gave my son unique gifts and skills to use.

Cling to the intention that your children will be responsible, that they'll choose the right friends, honor authority figures, and that they'll be able to handle rejection and failure right along with success with a hope-filled and humble attitude; that they'll display good management skills over their finances, use self-control at all times, and be willing to delay gratification.

Embrace the intention that they can manage their emotions well, care for their body in a healthy and appropriate manner, and pursue their passions in a Godly way. Clutch the intention that they are capable of recognizing and responding appropriately when temptation is on the prowl in their lives. Believe that they are capable of walking in and exercising faith in their own lives and that they can hear the voice of God clearly. Grasp the intention that they will live their life in Godly, righteous pursuits.

Create a Plan

To lead with intention and vision, create a plan. Sometimes we find ourselves daydreaming instead of honoring a cherished and wise vision with forward motivation and dedication.

You need a plan or course of action to sustain change and reach a goal. Slow yourself down. Take inventory of where you and your child are. Get a strong picture of where you want to be and where you want your child to be. The time it takes to do this, deeply committing yourself to the future you want, is time well-spent. To achieve any worthwhile goal, you and your child need to "own" your strengths, your skills, and your talents. You and your child also need to come face-to-face with obstacles and with your own God-given aptitude for overcoming them.

Here's a very common example. Many parents want to experience less stress and enjoy more quality time with their children. How can a parent make this vision into a reality? Start by taking inventory: When are you busiest? When do you have down time? What tasks, activities and options can be scaled back or removed? Are the actions and energies you expend bringing you the consequences you desire? Just a few targeted questions like these can help you realize different options that you may have.

Move forward when the inventory is complete. Start with a clear mental picture of what "more time with your children" looks like. Since the picture is your end goal, re-visit it throughout the day. Of course, your plan must be realistic for your family's lifestyle.

When you've developed a viable plan, stick to your guns! Don't check emails, read the mail, return phone calls, or do anything else that clutters your time. Be present with your children. Help them with homework, play a game with them, take them for a walk, read with them. Do "whatever it is" and have fun, uninterrupted by other "shoulds" (I should have worked longer, I should have run errands, I should have cleaned the house). You'll soon develop peace of mind, seeing that your family is happier and you are happier. And you can be proud because you created a realistic and specific plan that you didn't allow the hustle and bustle of the day to sabotage. Your initiative brings you and your family joy, peace, and contentment. You are a person of power with brilliant ideas, plans and goals.

Darius Goes West: Living Life with Intention as a True Visionary

I recently had the privilege of meeting Darius Weems, his right hand man, Logan Smalley, driver Daniel Epting, comic relief Jason Hees and a gaggle of their other vivacious, caring friends. Darius has Duchenne Muscular Dystrophy, a fatal form and the number one genetic killer of children. Darius and his friends decided one day that they should make a film depicting their journey from Athens, Georgia to Los Angeles, California with the ultimate goal of having MTV "pimp his ride" (wheelchair). Darius had never gone away from home and was obviously limited physically, but he and his friends were given a vision and followed through with it. They created a plan, raised funds for the trip, overcame numerous obstacles along the way and were very specific, time-oriented and realistic. The goal challenged their everyday norm, stretched them as humans, and brought them to new sights and life experiences. Not easy to do, but certainly attainable.

The end result was the multi-award winning documentary "Darius Goes West." The documentary has educated hundreds of thousands of people about Duchenne Muscular Dystrophy, raised money for research, inspired others to live out their dreams, and provided Darius and his friends with unforgettable experiences.

Darius doesn't view life from a perspective of limitation but of countless opportunities to live life to the fullest while he can. He doesn't worry about the past or the future. He lives, enjoys and makes the most of every moment. Darius and his friends are modern-day visionaries who daily reap the benefits of the vision and intention they have sown. I highly recommend the film to you; it will bring tears of laughter and poignancy to your eyes. (If you want to learn more about Darius and his mission, you can go to www.dariusgoeswest.com.)

I must note here that Darius was brought up by his single mother, Jamie Robinson, in the "projects" of Athens, Georgia. When speaking with him one day, I asked about his mom. Darius's eyes lit up; he beamed with love. The movie is replete with interactions between Darius and his mom. The scenes show just how vital a parent-child relationship is and how they complement and enhance each other's lives.

Ms. Robinson has my utmost respect. She has raised a young man with an eager desire to make the most of every moment and experience life to the fullest in spite of limitations. Darius is a world changer. This young man could be independently wealthy from the proceeds of the film but he elects to retain the life he has and donate all the money to research for Duchenne. He has been quoted as saying, *"Scientists are close to finding treatment or a cure for DMD, I know it won't happen in time to save me, but I want to prevent the next generation with this disease from going through what I have."*

You, your child and family can do the impossible, too. Live your life with vision and purpose. The results will be amazing.

Intention and Vision for Your Child's Life

If you hold tightly to your intention for your children, they will naturally develop their strengths, skills, talents, gifts and abilities. God has called each of them to a particular purpose. As a parent living with intention for your child, maintain high expectations. When you do this, children naturally aim for your target; they know you have faith in them to succeed.

It's scriptural to have intention and vision. In 1 Corinthians 9:24-28 Paul talked about running his race and finishing it. The apostle viewed his life as having a starting point and a concluding place. In Psalm 33:13-15, David talks about how the Lord formed each of our hearts and considers everything we do.

It is ultimately your child's job to determine what the purpose, passion and vision is for his life. Your job is to create the intention so that when your child or teen is old enough, he will have it. He will be able to see past limitations and mistakes and use available resources to get where he needs to go. God will guide him along the way. Mistakes will be stepping stones toward learning and growth, not something to dwell on or provide a rationale for quitting.

As a child filled with inner wealth, your child will not look to others as a means of comparison or rivalry but as a means to find mutual support and a helpful network. When children and teens live in their God-given inner wealth, they don't worry about what others have or whether others are better; they simply enjoy who they are in the moment, reaching farther every time they try something.

The Lord is good and loves us with an enduring love (Psalm 100:5). Trust in the Lord that his vision and plan for your child's life is the best plan and that it will foster the desires of their hearts. (Psalm 37:3-6)

Chapter Summary

In this chapter we have learned that *Parenting with Power, Love and Sound Mind* means leading from a perspective of strength and seeing the glass as half full. In this light, children and teens with intensity are seen as glorious gifts to the world with vision and purpose. To fight for our intense children's victories, we must be prepared to battle anyone or anything that places or sows negativity or failure into the portfolios of our children. We will "Shamu" our children into success and see from the eyes and perspective of the toll taker. In addition, we will hold proper agendas and intentions for our children so they can live out their God-given purpose and vision.

Questions for Reflection

1. What intense qualities exist in your child that can be viewed as their strengths, skills, talents and abilities?
2. How can you deepen and develop these God-given gifts?
3. What is currently in your child or teenager's portfolio? What is good in the portfolio and what needs a little work?
4. Pay attention for an entire day or two to the words and attitudes you sow into your child. Where are you going right and what do you need to get busy fixing?
5. What are some things that you currently view as negative that with a little perspective change can locate the positive (think toll taker)?
6. Identify ways you can "Shamu" your child into success. Be creative and think outside the norm.
7. Identify positive agendas and intentions you're currently holding for your child or teen. Write them down or share them.

Prayer for Today

Lord, thank You for entrusting me with an intense child. I am so grateful to be able to guide and raise this child for You. I ask that You give me the strength to find the positives in each and every situation I am in with my child and in my own life. Please open my eyes, mind, heart, ears and spirit to see ways in which I can sow blessing into my child. I thank You that I will parent vigorously to sow godliness, gloriousness and greatness into my child's portfolio. With You by my side, I will parent with proper agendas and intention and reap the benefits of all my hard work and effort. I pray and love You in the Name of Jesus. Amen

TRANSFORMING COMMUNICATION AND INTERACTION WITH YOUR CHILD OR TEEN

This section includes specific methods of conversation to have with your child to build up their inner wealth and inner strength. In this section you will learn the four major recognitions, developed by Howard Glasser, as key components to the Nurtured Heart Approach™. You will memorize and share these recognitions consistently with your child or teen. The recognitions are Active, Experiential, Pro-Active and Creative. The final chapter in this section pulls together the use of all the recognitions to transform your world! All of these recognitions are built on the information you have learned in earlier chapters- guard your heart and mind, watch your words, reap and sow good things into your child's portfolio, keep a positive perspective at all times, and parent with high expectations and intentions.

Chapter 5:
Active Recognition:
Unconditional Acceptance
(Picture-Oriented Parenting)

"Kids go where there is excitement. They stay where there is love."

(Zig Ziglar)

While I was meditating on what Active Recognition really is, I had a few thoughts that I would like to share. Active Recognition is really the Biblical principle of not judging others (Matthew 7:1, James, 4:11, Luke 6:37 and Romans 2:1) and walking in truth and love. Active Recognition is a communication strategy that allows you to verbally share exactly what you see a person doing with no bias, attitude, opinion or judgment. It is the most basic of the recognitions because it simply acknowledges a person for just being uniquely who they are. How powerful! Allowing your child to know that she is noticed for doing what comes naturally, similar to Shamu, tells her she is indisputably and unconditionally valued.

Thinking of the story of Jesus and the woman who was caught in the act of adultery, I love how Jesus handled the situation. While the Pharisees tried to use the adulterous woman as a means to catch Jesus, He actually turned the story around and caught them (John 8:2-11). Now, you may say to me that the story is not really about judging but more about forgiveness. I agree, but what I would like you to notice is a group of men were standing in judgment of Jesus. When called to task by Jesus to cast the first stone if they were innocent, they couldn't. Every Pharisee left that place because all of them had committed the same act as the woman, possibly even with the woman. Jesus, the only person who could legitimately judge her, unconditionally loved her, forgave her and sent her on her way to live differently. Jesus gave the woman her dignity and self respect. When you recognize, fellowship, encourage and share with your child, work hard to remove as much judgment (positive and negative) as possible so the full effect of what you are saying can be absorbed without filters.

A child came to my office overflowing with sadness. It was leaking from every pore of her body. We engaged in a conversation about how wonderful a friend she was because she was able to be thoughtful and honor a friend's confidentiality, an attribute that is usually difficult for an average teenager with juicy information. Although I shared with her the obvious characteristics she was displaying, her love for herself was so lacking that she couldn't receive the information. What this told me was that I needed to Actively Recognize her; give her irrefutable information about herself to start the process of instilling inner wealth and inner strength. I changed my character-rich descriptions to comments like these:

"Jillian, I see you sitting there with a yellow top, giving me good eye contact. I notice you sitting calmly and doodling with your notebook paper and pen. Your hair is in a braid today and you are wearing your glasses."

This may seem very odd or silly but it works. When you Actively Recognize your child or teen, she will internalize what you say as acceptance and value for who she is. It is a wonderful way to start building transformation.

Definition of Active Recognition

Active Recognition takes a verbal "snapshot" of a situation and describes it without judgment or evaluation. It is a joyful play-by-play account of recent or current actions or feelings. It's an acknowledgment that something great is happening or has just happened. Active Recognition is given in the here and now. Liveliness and fellowship radiate from the speaker's verbal and non-verbal communication.

Active Recognition phrases often begin with "I notice" or "I see." Be honest and genuine with Active Recognitions. Use them liberally throughout the day. "I see you playing with your blocks pretending to be a builder."

Purpose of Active Recognition

Active Recognition underlines "successes" that may not be obvious to your child. Your goal is to have your child's success resonate with him or her in an indisputable way. Active Recognition is especially helpful for children who see themselves mostly in a negative light (e.g., kids who frequently get into trouble, who are depressed or struggling with low self-worth).

Children who view themselves as different, displeasing or as troublemakers have a difficult time believing in their greatness when someone tries to invalidate their faulty pre-programmed belief system. When someone says something good about such children, their negative belief systems tells them to discount any information that indicates they're actually quite good. To get around this errant defensiveness, it's important to speak truthful, indisputable statements that document each of their successes.

Active Recognition lets parents, teachers and other caregivers help a child feel loved and cherished just for being who they are. With Active Recognition, a child begins to feel, deep down, that she is valued, loved and special simply because she exists and does what she loves.

Active Recognition Puts Power in Your Hands

Active Recognition empowers you to capture an ordinary moment and make it feel, to your child, like an extraordinary personal success. To do this, describe to your child what you see him doing while he's doing something good, and allow him the pleasure of feeling important and memorable. Whenever an adult takes time-out of her routine, stops what she's doing and genuinely acknowledges a child, the youngster's portfolio fills with positive pictures about who he is. Helping your child feel loved, valued and cared for is much more important than any other "perk" you can give him. When he knows in his heart that he's special (as a result of the positive information you provide to him via Active Recognitions), he'll begin to behave like someone who is special and will live and thrive out of that portfolio.

Feelings are Important

Active Recognitions teach your child that feelings are a natural part of who he is and that he should embrace them. Tell him he's expected to feel sad, mad, glad, tired, and bored. Feelings should be acknowledged and felt. The key to success for your child is to teach him how to recognize his feelings and embrace them in ways that are healthy and productive.

Adults and children who are in touch with their feelings have personal power over their responses. Feelings are a big part of each of us. They signal to us what's going on inside and help us make decisions about how to respond. In our culture, many have learned to keep our emotions to ourselves or to deny them altogether. I've spent time with children and teens who have told me they hate to cry because it shows weakness. Others have told me they were confident they didn't have feelings and were just numb. Still others said that when they experience an intense emotion, they try to push it away.

I believe children have learned from the world that their emotional states are not acceptable and should disappear. Well-meaning parents have told them, "Suck it up," "Stop crying. You're fine," "Why do you feel like that? It was no big deal," "You're just being silly," and "Stop acting so angry — no one is bothering you."

Active Recognitions acknowledge feelings. It's important to let your children own their feelings. They need to recognize and be in touch with them. When children, teens and adults deny their feelings, the emotions reveal themselves in other ways. People will use food, drugs and alcohol, self-injurious behavior, extreme exercise, and other things to deal with emotional issues. People who squelch their feelings tend to struggle with anxiety and depression.

Give your children opportunities to talk about feelings. Show them you're paying attention; acknowledge their feelings. Help them by giving a name to every feeling, and support them unconditionally through intense emotions. If your child is in touch with her emotions, she'll readily recognize what she's feeling. She'll give herself permission to experience the emotion and then move on to the next success. People who are skilled at being in touch with their feelings navigate the world with greater confidence and ease. They tend to see challenges as opportunities and steer clear of high-risk, unhealthy and addictive behaviors.

Here is a Range of Typical Emotions Experienced by All Ages. Teach Healthy Acknowledgment and Expression of Emotions and A Child Will Navigate the World with Confidence:

Amazed, confused, carefree, ecstatic, guilty, suspicious, excited, wise, angry, hysterical, frustrated, sad, confident, embarrassed, happy, mischievous, disgusted, frightened, enraged, ashamed, sweet, cautious, smug, depressed, overwhelmed, hopeful, lonely, love-struck, wonderful, wise, jealous, bored, surprised, anxious, shocked, peaceful, zeal, content, joyful, brave, focused, peaceful, etc.

The next time you see your child experiencing an emotion, don't wait until the emotion passes or allow the emotion to carry them to the point where a rule is broken. Take the opportunity to make the emotion a moment of success: "I see you're upset that I can't take you to the store right now. You are allowing yourself to feel your feelings and are controlling your anger." Doing this gives your child permission to feel his feelings and to know he can manage and navigate difficult times. When this sense of mastery is internalized, your child will be more prepared every time a situation arises that causes him distress. The more he feels success when handling intense emotions, the more powerfully he will say no to peer pressure, drugs, alcohol and other destructive and dangerous paths for his life.

Living by the Spirit is more important

Although feelings are important and we need to teach our children all about feelings, we also need to teach our children to live by the spirit. We are people that live in a body and have a soul (mind, will and emotions) but we are spirit. We should not be guided by our feelings or subject to the desires of our body; we should follow and learn to cultivate listening to our spirit and teaching our children to do the same. We also learned in Chapter 3 the importance of words. Please, tell your children to be truthful and knowledgeable with their feelings but help them also understand the value of words. As Christians we are to listen to the small still voice, the Holy Spirit within us. We are also commanded to live and walk by faith. It is important to teach our children to do the same. They must confess that no matter what they feel, the Word says they will be victorious overcomers.

Actively Recognize Young Children

Most young children will bask in the glow of Active Recognitions. But if you have a child who is hardwired to a negative impression of herself, or who has a difficult time accepting positive statements, you may incorrectly assume right away that the Nurtured Heart Approach™ isn't working. In my experience and the experience of other colleagues in the field, this is simply not the case.

What is happening is that your child is not used to positive statements, so she doesn't know how to handle them. She's afraid of shifting to a new perspective. Since her comfort zone is in the negative, she'll do whatever it takes to get back to the usual routine in her life, the one that insists, "I only get attention when I'm being a stinkbug."

Don't fall into the trap. Remain confident that you're following God's plan for your child. Stay strong and amplify your Active Recognitions until she finally "gets it." And remember to give zero energy to negative behaviors; a simple "reset" or time-out should be all your child receives. *Follow this rule: The more intense the child, the more intensely you need to follow the approach!*

Actively Recognizing Teens

I've worked with countless teenagers and their parents. Every time I introduce the approach to parents, they laugh and tell me their teen is going to think they are "nuts" for talking to them in the new language.

Teenagers are especially fun to use the approach on. If you do it like their life depended on it (and it does!), the change you see in them will be dramatic.

My philosophy is to tell your teenager the truth but in a way that shows your personality and confirms that you're not going to back down. Here's a prime example: When your teen questions the reasoning behind all of the compliments and acknowledgements, say "I know it seems odd and a bit silly, but I realized that I was spending too much time telling you all that was going bad and not enough time on all the great things you do. I like this way better, so I'm going to stick with it."

Recognizing Teens with Hardened Hearts

The majority of the teens I see have been in trouble with the law, have been involved with drugs and alcohol, and have refused to follow the rules their parents set down. This approach will work for troubled, intense teens but the results may look a bit different at first. As with the young children mentioned in above examples, teens will discount you at first — and they may even make fun of you— but in my experience, they'll sit there looking comatose or incredulous, and not know what to make of the new information you're telling them about their documented areas of greatness.

Troubled teens have hardened hearts, so you'll need to accept on faith that they are internalizing the new information. To combat their hard hearts, pray, stand in faith, be immensely present with them, and add more detail and enthusiasm to your words. It may feel odd or funny at first but you'll get used to it. As soon as you begin to see a glimmer of belief and pride in your teen's eyes, believe me: you'll be eager to stay in the game!

Examples

Before I provide a list of examples for a variety of age groups, it's important to remember what Active Recognitions are **not**.

Active Recognitions Are _Not_:

Questions; "Are you playing with your dolls?"

Judgmental statements; "I can't believe you are playing so quietly." "I like the way…"

Offered when children are behaving inappropriately; "I see you hitting your sister."

Nor are they typical adult responses; All too often, when adults share their kudos with a child they say things like, "nice shot," "well done," "good job," "thank you" or "awesome."

With active recognitions, you simply say out loud what the child is doing, with enjoyment in your voice and body language. Take time to note both actions and emotions. Be specific: notice and describe what you see.

Here is how I would change the adult responses above into Active Recognitions:

Instead of "Nice shot" at the soccer game, say: "I see you running as hard as you can, maneuvering the ball as you go. You are totally on fire."

Instead of "Well done" for taking out the trash, say: "I notice that you're frustrated with doing the chore but I see you continuing to pick up the garbage and take it out."

Instead of "Good job" playing restaurant, say: "I see you setting the table, taking orders from your dolls, and making sure they're seated comfortably. You seem thrilled."

Instead of saying "Thank you" for putting things away, say: "You took off your coat and your backpack and put them in the closet neatly."

Active Recognitions are simply a description of the positive things you see going on with your children. Watch, describe and document what you see aloud as if you're describing the scene and activity for a blind companion. Become a live, audio-visual camera for your children and capture their successful, motivated, creative, obliging behaviors and even how well they handle their emotions during frustrating times whenever you see greatness there.

Active Recognitions (Picture-Oriented Parenting)

Share with your child <u>exactly</u> what you see them doing. Give a detailed description of the child and what they're doing or feeling.

This strategy creates success out of everyday moments and allows the child to value himself for exactly who he is in the moment without any expectations being placed on him.

This recognition will also increase a sense of value, attention and love from you for your child and begin the process of transformation by teaching her the power of living in the present moment.

More Examples

Remember to remain in the here and now. Give recognitions honestly and liberally. Your children will learn to see ordinary moments as moments of success and they'll discover they can handle strong emotions. "I can't" will no longer be an issue, because they are doing it right now and you have recognized them for it!

"Melissa, I noticed all of the effort you put into the fundraiser. You are an advocate."

"Jeannie, I see you creating ribbons in an array of colors for all of the causes you feel so strongly about."

"Tyler, I notice you putting your trucks and cars in two separate lines as if they're waiting at a toll booth. The trucks are arranged biggest to littlest. The cars are matched by color."

"Diane, I see that you are sad. I appreciate that you're handling your strong feelings so well."

"Jerome, you're angry right now because you can't get the puzzle pieces to fit right, but you're sticking with it to make it work. That shows great concentration and dedication."

Chapter Summary

Active Recognition is all about non-judgmentally sharing with your child what you see and hear them doing that pleases you. It doesn't include bias, questions, attitudes or pre-conceived notions. It is the first of the Recognitions to use and the most basic. It allows your children to digest the notion that they are being noticed and valued unconditionally just for doing what comes naturally and for being uniquely themselves. Use Active Recognitions throughout the day.

Points for Reflection

1. Take time to Actively Recognize your child or teen numerous times throughout the day.
2. Write down or talk about some of the things your children or teens are already doing that will allow you to Actively Recognize them.
3. Develop a plan to teach your child feelings and to live by the Spirit.
4. Practice Actively Recognizing yourself or someone else to get used to the idea of sharing non-judgmental, descriptive interaction.

Prayer for Today

Lord, thank You for giving me the ability to take time to Actively Recognize my children for being the exclusive version of who You created them to be. I ask You to help me notice my children more and more when they are just being present as themselves. Please give me the wisdom, knowledge, utterance and discernment to use Active Recognitions and healthy expression of feelings. Thank You for being a God who is gracious and merciful. I pray this in the Name of Jesus, Amen

Chapter 6:
Experiential Recognition:
Character Value and Education

"The colossal misunderstanding of our time is the assumption that insight will work with people who are unmotivated to change. Communication does not depend on syntax, or eloquence, or rhetoric, or articulation but on the emotional context in which the message is being heard. People can only hear you when they are moving toward you, and they are not likely to when your words are pursuing them. Even the choicest words lose their power when they are used to overpower. Attitudes are the real figures of speech."
(Edwin H. Friedman)

Experiential Recognition (Values and Character-Oriented Parenting)

As we mentioned in the previous chapter, "thank you," "good job," "awesome" and all the other ways we use to express appreciation to our children will not work with *Parenting with Power, Love and Sound Mind.* You need to press on and follow those words with descriptive language of what you appreciate, see and value in your child or teen. In Active Recognition, we simply described what we saw a child feeling and doing. In Experiential Recognition, we add the genuine and truthful characteristics we see our child or teen displaying. Experiential Recognition allows our child or teen to receive firsthand experience of what they're doing so they'll recognize and internalize their good and acceptable qualities.

The Apostle Paul rarely, if ever, used just a simple "Bless them Father" or "Thank you" when speaking to God in his prayers for others. Paul was very descriptive in what he wanted people to receive from God, how he wanted them to live their lives, and what his expectations were. (Ephesians 1:15-22, 3:14-20,Philippians 1:9-11, Colossians 1:9-14, 1Thessalonians 3:12-13)

Just as Paul was descriptive in his prayers, you need to be descriptive when speaking with your children. The more you share the characteristics, values, traits, skills, talents and abilities you want them to display, the more they'll exhibit those qualities.

The Christian life is based on our acceptance and reliance on God, Jesus and the Holy Spirit. Daily, living out the life of the triune God requires putting into action His character values. Your child and teen cannot learn these valuable lessons of life without you drawing attention to them and descriptively sharing times when these positive traits are present. The passage that most clearly denotes this expected character is Galatians 5: 22-23:

"But the fruit of the Spirit is love, joy, peace, patience, kindness, goodness, faithfulness, gentleness and self-control. Against such things there is no law."

The Scriptures emphasize the importance of good character in the Bible. It is written that God knows and desires excellent wisdom in one's inner being (Psalm 51:6). Even children are known by their pure conduct and actions (Proverbs 20:11). Those with good character welcome truth. (Luke 8:15)

Tom and Lynette wanted their nine-year-old triplets to be more cooperative. The girls were fighting a bit too much, not sharing, and generally just being mean to each other. Tom and Lynette were running around the house like chickens with their heads cut off trying to get each young lady to behave. Car rides involved constant threats to pull over, stop the vehicle and intervene in their constant squabbling.

I taught Tom and Lynette to start noticing even the shortest times the girls were sitting quietly, playing nicely, doing something that displayed kindness or generosity. As soon as Tom and Lynette started showering the girls with Experiential Recognitions about the girls' ability to cooperate, divide up the spoils of toys and candy and be gentle with one another in words and actions, the triplets stopped behaving badly. The parents began to take delight in advising the girls of their great pleasure in seeing them sitting and keeping their hands to themselves and about how inquisitive, artistic and creative they were. When the girls realized that the true deliciousness of fellowship with mom and dad was in their power, they changed their behaviors from negative to positive.

Definition of Experiential Recognition

An Experiential Recognition is a "freeze frame" account of a recent or current action. It includes describing and emphasizing the value or character quality that you observed your child naturally displaying. A value is a closely-held belief. As Christian parents, we're filled with hundreds of values we want our children to internalize and hold dear. We want them to be peaceful, patient, resilient, faithful, slow to anger, quick to listen, responsible, exercisers of good judgment and to be joyful and selfless.

Unfortunately, as we saw earlier, parents tend to teach these values to their children at the worst possible time: when children are *mis*behaving, doing the opposite of the value we want to see in them. For example, a parent might say, "Why are you behaving like this? You need to be a better listener and sit still in your chair so that Pastor is respected." Or "How come you always forget to take a shower, brush your teeth and get dressed for church?" or the ever-popular, "Stop eating so fast. Get your elbows off the table and use your fork. Mind your table manners."

These statements are obviously well-meaning attempts to get children to do the right thing. The problem is that they unintentionally reinforce negative behavior. If you're doling out high levels of emotion, time, energy and conversation at times when things are going wrong, you'll get more of the same behavior because that's where the payoff is. The correct time to offer energy and enthusiasm is when children are engaged with us in a positive way. That's when to teach the qualities you want to see grow.

Our children come to us as blank slates: they need our help to learn values and character qualities. By design, they can't evaluate their own experiences. If we acknowledge the positive character qualities they exhibit in the moment while they're occurring naturally, we help them learn to recognize and honor them as we do.

Children are receptive to learning life lessons in positive ways and will absorb what you say. When your children are engaged in what you're saying, they're downloading the information into their souls.

So the next time you see your child modeling a behavior with a positive value or character quality that you appreciate and want to ensure becomes part of his portfolio, share it descriptively and with high energy. Use the value and character word you're noticing and do it with excitement and lots of delicious relationship energy. For example, "That shows good cooperation," "You're behaving very responsibly," "Right now you're showing self control," and "Wow, way to use your faith!"

A good way to phrase Experiential Recognitions is to start sentences with "I love," "I like," "I'm pleased," "I appreciate," "I am so blessed," or "I'm thrilled." When you use phrases like these, you're letting your child know they're engaging in a behavior or exhibiting a quality that makes you happy. Your high verbal and non-verbal energy levels will seal the deal and your child will work hard to create the same scenario again and again.

Experiential Recognition (Value and Character- Oriented Parenting)

Use high energy verbal and non-verbal cues to let children know when they are naturally engaging in behaviors you want them to incorporate into their lives. This will teach them values while they are actively engaged in doing them.

This kind of recognition builds inner wealth and strong portfolios of character education, confidence, assertiveness and a sense of wellbeing.

Purpose

The purpose of Experiential Recognition is to recognize and show keen excitement for any discernible degree of a positively-valued character trait your child or teen exhibits. This teaches them to demonstrate character skills and closely-held values using their own good judgment. When a child is recognized as displaying valuable traits without having been prodded to do so, it's extremely empowering. The child hears internal applause which builds inner wealth, greatness, a moral compass and confidence.

Some Helpful Values to Teach Your Children

Courage, faithfulness, humility, resourcefulness, perseverance, self- discipline, wisdom, work, devotion, faith, holiness, joyfulness, obedience, prayerfulness, repentance, thankfulness, compassion, forgiveness, honesty, friendliness, love, kindness and unselfishness.

(More characteristics and values to build up children can be found in the Appendix.)

Our children are on loan to us. We must teach them how to handle life's successes and failures for the day when they'll be beyond our control and navigating the world on their own. The more we share the values and character qualities we see them displaying, the larger their internal "tool box" will be from which to choose as they face life situations. The more filled the tool box, the greater the likelihood of victory.

Examples of Experiential Recognition

"I'm very pleased to see you eating your vegetables and asking for more. That's very responsible and healthy eating."

"I love that you're cooperating with your brother and putting away all of the toys together. Great team work and thoughtfulness."

"I so admire the way you answered that difficult question with a clear mind."

"I appreciate the good choice you made to speak thoughtfully."

"I'm pleased with you helping me set the table. You're a great example to your younger siblings. You're a hard worker and a magnificent helper."

"You took great care of those butterflies before they came out of their cocoons. You were trustworthy in caring for them and showed focus and determination to see them come out safely."

"I am so grateful that you can tell jokes to make people feel better. You have a sense of humor that is glorious!"

"I love the way you broke the candy bar into three equal pieces. You were very fair."

"I'm blessed to see you flourish and exceed expectations in your Bible study."

"I appreciate your desire to help me at the pancake breakfast fundraiser. You're considerate, cooperative and generous with your time."

Chapter Summary

This Chapter continues the language of *Parenting with Power, Love and Sound Mind* by teaching you how to instill positive character qualities and values in your child or teen when they are displaying these great traits. By teaching your children or teens when they are being patient, responsible or cooperative, they internalize and adopt that characteristic as their own. Following the law of reaping and sowing, you will get more of the values and wisdom your child or teen displays when you descriptively advise them with jubilant voice and actions what you see and hear them doing.

Points for Reflection

1. Take time to Experientially Recognize your child or teen numerous times throughout the day. Be descriptive and generous with your communication.
2. Write down or talk about some of the things your child or teen is already doing that will allow you to Experientially Recognize them.
3. Develop a plan to help you prioritize the character qualities you want to teach your child or teen.
4. Practice Experientially Recognizing yourself or someone else to get used to the idea of providing abundant and sumptuous dialogue for positive character and value traits.

Prayer for Today

Lord, thank You for giving me the eyes to see and the ability to take time to Experientially Recognize my children for all of the positive character qualities they display. I ask You to help me notice and prompt my spirit to share Godly values present in my child or teen. Please give me the wisdom, knowledge, utterance and discernment to use Experiential Recognitions and every possible opportunity to teach these valuable lessons. Thank You for Your presence and never ending source of strength in my life. I pray this in the Name of Jesus, Amen.

Chapter 7:
Proactive Recognition:
Rules for Life

"Feelings of worth can flourish only in an atmosphere where
individual differences are appreciated, mistakes are tolerated,
communication is open, and rules are flexible — the kind of atmosphere
that is found in a nurturing family." (Virginia Satir)

We have covered how to use Active Recognition to demonstrate unconditional acceptance. We have discussed Experiential Recognition to teach the characteristics, values and qualities that are expected and honored in your family. Now we will be talking about how to teach the rules to your child with Proactive Recognition. This may seem hard to believe, but you will actually teach the rules to your child when they are NOT breaking the rules.

Not all of the rules in scripture were taught when people were misbehaving. Moses taught the Israelites the Ten Commandments when they were NOT breaking the rules. Jesus taught the multitudes and his disciples when they were sitting quietly and listening to Him. When Jesus fed the 5000, the Bible declares that Jesus had compassion for the crowd. He fed them bread and fishes so they could be present with him and go home with their physical, mental and spiritual needs met (Matthew 14:13-21). People were present, paying attention and wanting to learn. They were engaged. Notice, too, that biblical rules are very simple and start with "no" or "do not." God knew what he was doing when he made rules that start with No: "Thou shalt not." Keep it simple and uncomplicated so there is no gray area (Exodus 20:2-17, Ephesians 4:29-32).

Teaching the rules when your child or teen is fully tuned in is helpful because they're present with you. What do I mean by that? Think of a time when someone criticized you. Were you gleefully thrilled to hear their wisdom, or were you preparing a rebuttal, wishing to get out of there, or just plain not listening? When I ask people in my seminars this question, very rarely do they say they enjoyed the critical discussion. The bottom line is that it is easier and more rewarding for all parties to teach the rules when the rules are NOT being broken.

I once worked with a family of a four-year-old child who seemed to have some sticky fingers and a great ability to tell stories. His parents could not figure out where or how this young pre-schooler learned to steal and lie. They were so despondent about the situation because they were getting consistent reports about this behavior from his grandparents, day care providers and the owner of the local corner store who saw some bubble gum go into this little guy's chubby hands and then into his pocket.

How did we fix this dire situation? I told the parents to begin sharing with him in descriptive, powerful and delightful ways when he was NOT stealing or lying. The turnabout was almost instantaneous. If this little guy was sharing about his day, his parents would share the characteristics they saw in his conversation and thank him for not lying and breaking that rule. When he walked around the house, they thanked him for not stealing. This quickly translated to the little boy that he was able to control his behaviors and, by not breaking the rules, he was lavished with love.

Proactive Recognition (Rules-Oriented Parenting)

Proactive Recognition is all about rules, rules, rules — but with a *Parenting with Power, Love and Sound Mind* twist. Traditional parenting teaches rules to your children when they misbehave. Now that you're wise to that upside-down parenting strategy, you're parenting with positivity and intention. You're sowing positive energy into your child and getting lots of positive energy in return. Let's keep that momentum going by teaching children the rules when they AREN'T breaking them.

"Yikes! Is she crazy?" I can hear you saying, "This is gonna be tough." I promise if you're following the approach diligently, this will get easier as time goes on. Stick to your intention for your child! Remember, you're learning a new mindset and language. It takes time, but you have a warrior spirit when it comes to your child, and you are more than a conqueror and can do ALL things through Christ.

Example: You're getting ready for dinner. Your two children are quietly doing their homework at the kitchen table. A Proactive Recognition to one child would be, "I so appreciate that you're not rocking in your chair. That shows self control." And to the second, "I'm blessed to see you not calling your brother names, teasing him, or interrupting him while he's working. That shows kindness and consideration."

Purpose

In Proactive Recognition, recognize when things go right and when rules **aren't** being broken. Comment immediately and energetically whenever you see appropriate behavior from your children. Doing so promotes healthy personal power and self-control. It will teach the rules to children "proactively" (before a rule is broken) and allow for their successes to be spotlighted.

Proactive Recognition gives your child a sense of personal responsibility. He learns that he's directly responsible for his behavior and for the choices that he makes. You share with him that he's not breaking the rules on his own and that it comes naturally, that he didn't need you to intervene and gain control of a deteriorating situation. Proactive Recognition shows your children they can make wise choices and experience resounding success without someone lecturing, nagging, or warning.

When you help your children recognize all the times they aren't breaking rules, you help them learn they can make wise choices without you and that they can trust their own spirits and voices. This will come in handy when you're not around and someone says, "Hey, wanna try a cigarette?" or anything else that goes against what your child knows to be appropriate behavior. When your child trusts his own voice and gets sufficient energy from you, he makes smarter choices, wants to follow rules, and has confidence in what he's saying and doing at all times. He is walking in power, love and sound mind!

Another purpose of Proactive Recognition is to share the rules with your children so they will know them. When a parent knows the rules and the kids know the rules, and everyone **knows** that everyone in the house knows the rules, wiggle room for breaking a rule becomes virtually impossible. Your boundaries are crystal clear. "I appreciate that you're NOT hitting or teasing your sister" makes it obvious that hitting and teasing aren't tolerated in your home. Any attempt to buck the system results in a consequence (which I'll explain in chapters 10 and 11).

If you're in the habit of making a big deal of your child's inappropriate behaviors, use this form of recognition to help yourself extinguish the habit. Make a BIG deal when the rules are being followed, not when they're being broken. Dance, clap, cheer, twirl around, and sing! Communicate in any way you can "Yippee! The rules are not being broken! I am one happy person to see rules being followed."

Does My Child Need to Know Every Rule Before We Start?

No. As parents, you need to know the rules cold, but your children don't have to know them to use this approach. Your children probably already do know the rules if you've established appropriate interactions in your home and disciplined them in any way for not following them. You'll teach them the rules by sharing Proactive Recognitions with them. They'll learn as they go.

Sometimes I'm asked why parents should make a big deal of appropriate behavior and responses. If a child is doing what they need to do, that's what we expect, so why bother? I hope the above insight and previous chapters have answered the question. Take the time to notice when the rules are not being broken and you'll get more of appropriate behaviors. Your family will be transformed to living a peaceful, laugh-filled life. Your power will be used to applaud the good things you see, the rules that are not being broken, the values and character qualities that touch your heart.

Proactive Recognitions (Rule-Oriented Parenting)

Recognize times when your child is NOT breaking the rules.
The purpose of proactive recognition is to make the rules crystal-clear, to teach the rules in a manner more available to the child, and to instill personal power and self control.

Examples of Proactive Recognitions

Start proactive recognitions with "I like....I love....I appreciate ....I'm impressed....I'm proud.....I'm pleased" and "Thanks for....."

Remember! There are many times in the day when your child is following the rules. Take notice whenever it happens and you and your child will both feel better!

"Thank you for not misbehaving at the restaurant. You sat in your chair, with your feet on the ground, ate all of your dinner, and used good manners."

"I liked it when you didn't hit back or scream. You managed your feelings."

"I love it when you're considerate and don't interrupt me when I'm in the middle of something."

"I appreciate that you came home and did your homework right away. You could have gone out to play first, but you didn't. That shows responsibility and good judgment." (Proactive and Experiential together)

"Thanks for getting back in control of your strong feelings. You were really mad and you calmed yourself down. You could have stayed mad, but you chose not to."

"I'm so impressed that you went right upstairs, brushed your teeth, washed your face, and got ready for bed without complaining or starting a fight."

"I appreciate your calmness when you're not being aggressive."

"I'm so thrilled you can be mad and still stay in control of yourself and your words. You could have hit, spit or screamed and you did not. Great ability to follow the rules."

Chapter Summary

In this Chapter we discussed Proactive Recognition. This recognition allows you to teach the rules to your child or teen when they are following the rules. In other words, you lecture, sermonize and instruct when the rule is NOT being broken. Proactive Recognition allows your child to learn the rules in a more digestible manner: when they are present and interested in hearing what you have to say. Use this recognition frequently and you will have far less broken rules.

Points for Reflection

1. Take time to recognize your child or teen proactively numerous times throughout the day. Be very clear in describing the rule or rules that are NOT being broken.
2. Write down or talk about some of the things your child or teen is already doing that will allow you to recognize them proactively.
3. Devise a prioritized list of rules that you wish to teach to your child or teen when they are NOT happening.
4. Practice recognizing yourself or someone else proactively to get used to the idea of sharing descriptive interaction when rules are NOT being violated.

Prayer for Today

Lord thank You for giving me the ability to provide Proactive Recognitions to my child or teen. I am so grateful to You for showing me through this book that my child or teen is more present with me when we are engaged in healthy and safe communication. Teaching rules when they are not being broken is a strange concept, but I understand the power and learning lessons behind it. Give me eyes to see and ears to hear when rules are not being broken so that I can share with my child or teen all that is going right. I thank You Lord with all of my heart, in the Name of Jesus I pray, Amen.

Chapter 8:
Creative Recognition: Making Requests That Get Results

Creative Recognition (Requests for Success-Oriented Parenting)

Creative recognition is the means by which you teach your child that your requests mean business and must be honored. People of faith who came to Jesus and to the prophets of old would come expecting to receive. They were clear about what they needed and didn't beat around the bush. This is how you must be with your child so your requests are complied with and everyone receives what is in their best interest. Jesus and the prophets were no different. They spoke with authority. This influence you are using is specifically geared to get an easy task accomplished by your child or teen so you can lay on the recognitions and win the battle of instilling inner wealth and inner strength.

My favorite biblical story which reminds me of Creative Recognition is the widow who was losing everything. I like this story because it shows a request being met. It details the creativity of the Prophet Elijah and how he used what was available to bring success to this woman (1 Kings 17.7-15). Initially Elijah asked very politely and kindly for something to eat and drink, but when the widow advised him of her impoverished situation Elijah took over and told this woman what she needed to do. When the woman was obedient, she had more than enough food to feed herself, her sons and Elijah. The Prophet made a clear and easy request that allowed the woman to comply and be blessed.

Jesus did something similar for the Samaritan woman at the well. He made a simple request for water from her. He did this to engage her and impart to her the gift of everlasting life. Use Creative Recognition along the same vein as Jesus. Take the time to advise your child or teen to complete a likely-to-accomplish or easy task. This will allow them to receive your genuine and heartfelt accolades and step deeper into the pool of gloriousness, godliness and greatness.

I use Creative Recognition for children and teens in the same circumstance as the children who really need Active Recognition. Sometimes you have to help your children or teens see that they can please you and display good qualities. When they are deep in despair and doing a continual dance of negativity, you need to get serious, inventive and resourceful to win the battle of transformation.

Definition of Creative Recognitions

When you think of Creative Recognitions, think Shamu and remember: Shamu's trainer made him feel good for doing what came naturally; swimming back and forth in the pool. He continued "applauding" Shamu in ways the whale could appreciate while raising the rope. Over time, the whale was jumping higher than he would have had he lived in the open sea.

Creative Recognition allows you to make requests of your child in a clear and concise way that fosters compliance and success. As soon as you experience success with Creative Recognition, you can build on it in other ways. Instead of saying, "Would you please?".... "Could you please?".... or simply, "Please..." you'll now say "I need you to...." or "I want you to..." giving your child the distinct impression that your words aren't merely a suggestion or a request, but a command, marching orders.

I know what you're thinking. We've all been taught that good manners are important and that we need to instill them in our children. I agree completely! But we need to teach manners in a way that communicates appropriately with the child. When you make a request of your child that he is required to fulfill, using "could, would and please" implies that your child has a choice when actually he doesn't!

The veracity of this insight hit me like a ton of bricks one day. I asked my son Chandler, "Would you please turn off the television and start getting ready for bed while I finish checking my emails?" It was a simple request, and I expected he would comply.

I walked into the family room ten minutes later and there sat Chandler. He hadn't moved an inch. When I asked what was happening, Chandler — without skipping a beat and with innocent honesty — said to me, "Oh, mommy, I thought you were giving me an option. I didn't know I had to do it." I knew then my words had to count when I needed compliance.

By all means, teach your child to use good manners, but when it comes to setting your children on a course of action, state clearly and indisputably what it is you need in a loving, nurturing, respectful tone. This will still teach manners and walking in love, but it promotes understanding, too.

Examples:

• "I need you to pick up your dirty clothes and put them in the wash basket."

• "I want you to take a shower now."

• "I need you to stop reading and come to dinner now."

The requests are easy to understand and offer simple directions to follow. It's important to remember that as soon as a child does as you ask, you need to honor their success and heap on lots of recognition for their achievement. Equally important is the need to stay in the moment. One mishap, one inappropriate behavior shouldn't ruin the entire minute, hour or day. Stay in the moment and consider each of them another opportunity to create and instill success in your child.

If you're concerned that your child won't honor any request, don't worry. Consider the story below of Isaac and Michael and begin to make requests when your child is already in the act of doing what you want him to do. Remember to provide verbal and non-verbal cues to keep the flow of energy going in the right direction.

Recognize even the smallest success; a good choice, a right attitude, any small glimpse of a desired behavior. As with Shamu, you sometimes have to start with the rope on the ground before you can jump 25 feet into the air. Provide honest, genuine, descriptive praise when you see things moving in the right direction. It doesn't have to be perfection; just a small amount of movement is praiseworthy.

Purpose

Creative Recognition helps promote the clarity of requests, and helps eliminate the illusion of choice. This is especially important for children with negative portfolios or those who are used to receiving your energy from their non-compliance and non-cooperation. The implication of choice placed inside the brain of a child with a negative portfolio creates a compulsion in him or her to deny your request. This results in people labeling your child oppositional, defiant, non-compliant, difficult and uncooperative. If your child understands that he has no choice, and that they will be rewarded with positive energy for honoring the request, they'll comply.

Creative Recognition also "creates," as with Shamu, success for children who are so steeped in negativity that neither they, their parents, nor their caregivers can see anything else. Follow this rule every time you encounter an intense or challenging child. **Remember: "The more intense a child, the more intense the intervention needs to be."**

Isaac and Michael

Isaac is a six-year-old boy who was brought to me by his dad, Michael. Isaac's mom had recently died of cancer and Isaac was living out-of-state in a foster home until the authorities could locate Michael. Michael knew he had a son, but had never seen or interacted with him, at the request of the mother.

When Michael and his new wife learned that Isaac was living in foster care, they readily welcomed him into their home. Michael came to see me about six months later. His wife was pregnant and close to giving birth. Michael was concerned because Isaac was very "non-compliant" at school, at home, and everywhere else.

Isaac was, for obvious reasons, a very unhappy and angry little boy. I let Michael know that he would need to create success for Isaac. I said, "Isaac feels out of place and unsure. He needs to know that he is loved and valued by you and your wife." We brainstormed some ideas, I shared some stories Howard Glasser had told me, and Michael went home with some Creating Recognition ideas.

Two weeks later, Michael came back. He was ecstatic, telling me that Isaac was a completely different child. When the family sat together to eat, Michael took the opportunity to tell Isaac, just as Isaac was lifting his fork to his mouth, that he needed him to take a bite of his food. Isaac did it because he was already doing it. Michael then energized the behavior: "Isaac, that's great! You did exactly what I told you to do. That is being cooperative." Isaac received appreciation in that manner throughout dinner until they all burst into laughter. And ever since that one dinner, Isaac and Michael have been building a successful relationship. As soon as Isaac began to feel the warmth of success, he began to comply with more difficult requests, e.g. "I need you to do your homework."

Since Michael took the time to create success for Isaac and didn't give up on him, he was able to create inner wealth and a new portfolio for Isaac. He gave Isaac a sense of belonging, of being valued, and allowed Isaac to begin expressing with openness and honesty his intense emotions about losing his mother.

Remember, the more difficult the child, the more energy and creativity is needed to pull, drag and force the child into success.

Creative Recognition (Requests for Success-Oriented Parenting)

Creative Recognition allows for requests to be made in a clear and concise manner in order to create success.

The first purpose of Creative Recognition is to make certain the child knows what needs to happen and then supply them with a lot of positivity for complying. Another purpose is to provide moments of success for children where success is not obvious and again, to pour verbal and non-verbal positivity on the child. This instills clarity and allows opportunities for success to be spotlighted and celebrated.

Examples

"I need you to pick up your toys right now." Then follow up with: "I see you picking up the toys from the floor and putting them in the toy box. I like it when you do as I ask. You're being cooperative and helpful."

"I want you to turn off the television now." Then follow up with: "I'm so thrilled you turned off the television immediately. That's being very respectful to me."

"I need you to carry the mail inside and put it on the table." Then follow up with: "I see you heading toward the mailbox and appreciate that you're being a super helper to me right now."

"I want you to get the stain out of your rug." Then follow up with: "I see you getting the rug cleaner and doing what I asked. I know you're frustrated because the stain is tough and I appreciate you showing perseverance in getting it out."

When you use Creative Recognition, it's vital that your acknowledgments and recognitions be detailed and specific. You can't be general, or fail to use descriptive words, nor can you display negative verbal or non-verbal communication. This method only works if you have all of these areas in check.

Chapter Summary

Creative Recognitions were specifically designed to help you win the battle of instilling inner wealth and inner strength. This recognition gives you the opportunity to make easy or average requests (that are likely to be completed) of your child or teen. The requests and their completion by the child earn genuine and truthful congratulatory accolades. Use this recognition frequently and with an eye to the imaginative, inventive and resourceful.

Points for Reflection

1. Take time to recognize your child or teen creatively numerous times throughout the day.
2. Write down or talk about some of the things your child or teen is already doing that will allow you to recognize them creatively.
3. Devise some original and ingenious methods you can use to recognize your child or teen creatively.
4. Practice Creative Recognition on someone else to get used to the idea of using inspired requests to infuse inner wealth, inner strength, gloriousness, godliness and greatness.

Prayer for Today

Lord, thank you for giving me Creative Recognition to help me expose my children or teens to their gifts, talents, abilities and skills. Please help me tap into Your vast knowledge and creative source to generate original and helpful ways to make requests of my child or teen. Thank you for giving me eyes to see, ears to hear and an open heart ready to receive Your wisdom. I love and thank you with my whole being. I pray this prayer in the mighty name of Jesus.

Chapter 9:
Putting It All Together

"You are the light of the world. A city on a hill cannot be hidden.
Neither do people light a lamp and put it under a bowl. Instead they
put it on its stand, and it gives light to everyone in the house. In the
same way, let your light shine before men, that they may see your
good deeds and praise your Father in heaven." (Matthew 5:14-16)

Hooray!! You've made it through all of the recognitions. I am so proud of your ability to stick with the information in this book. You are a parent who is "wise as a serpent and gentle as a dove." You have all the power, compassion, tools and abilities to nurture, love and pursue the best possible life and outcome for your child or teen. Thank you for being diligent, patient, helpful and ready to do battle and win the war. Your unyielding, immovable and unbendable spirit to see your children thrive and achieve their God-given potential, vision and life's purpose is remarkably awe-inspiring.

Before we move on, I want to revisit briefly all of the recognitions we've just covered to keep them fresh in your mind. Active Recognition is the non-judgmental, unbiased description of your children or teens behaving just as they naturally would. The goal of Active Recognition is to allow your child or teen to soak in your unconditional love and value for him without his having to perform in any way. Experiential Recognition is used to teach character values that allow your child to develop strong inner wealth and inner strength as well as godliness, greatness and gloriousness. Proactive Recognition "lectures" (profoundly acknowledges) your child when the rules are NOT being broken. Finally, Creative Recognition is used to plunge your children into success by giving them requests that are typical and easy to accomplish. Shower your offspring with these recognitions every chance you get. This will bring about the transformation you seek.

As you use the recognitions please remember the foundation they were built on:

- the need to guard your heart, mind and words and fill all these areas of your life with what is trustworthy and noble;
- the principle of reaping and sowing good, appropriate and highly beneficial behaviors and attitudes;
- the notion of keeping a positive perspective in all circumstances;
- the desire to teach and train up your offspring with appropriate agendas and heartfelt intentions.

Putting It All Together

Use all of the recognitions regularly throughout the day. Combine them or use them individually. No matter which way you use them, always reflect the joy you feel with your child. You may notice, from the above examples, that there is frequently a deluge of "big words." This expands your children's vocabulary, helping them connect the dots from the action they're taking to the character-defining word they're portraying. It also sparks more creative energy and brain activity, helping you become a positive communicator. Don't be afraid to expand your own vocabulary in this way. It will benefit everyone in your family and environment to have more words with which to convey appreciation, observation of traits of greatness, and other positive interactions.

Offering dialogue for accomplishments, successes and observed rules may seem "silly" to you at first. I think most parents are skeptical to differing degrees at the outset. But it works, and it works powerfully! Don't be afraid to try it because it's outside your comfort zone or because it's just not how you do things. By giving it a try, I promise you'll notice an amazing difference in the peacefulness in your home and in the increasing level of love and appreciation that will exist in your family.

Frequently parents respond to their compliant kids with expressions like "Thank you," "Good job," "Awesome" and other quick, perfunctory means. There is no clarity in statements like these. Your youngest child isn't sure what, how, when or where they did whatever it was that elicited your statement. And vague acknowledgements don't teach a child about the character qualities and values or the appropriate behaviors they'll need to succeed in life. Adding *why* you're saying the words powerfully and emotionally implants into your child's soul a sense of accomplishment, triumph, values and necessary qualities. If you're having trouble breaking the habit of "thank you" and "good job," go ahead and say it, but then add some details; use descriptive words that burst with vibrant energy and information.

Be honest with recognitions. Genuinely recognize what's happening. That's the key to building inner wealth, trust and intimate relationship that lasts a lifetime.

As I address each strategy, please note again that you'll be working with your children when things are going well, not when they're misbehaving. You'll have to fight the tendency to "let sleeping dogs lie." In other words, you'll engage with your children when they're doing what you want: displaying good character, behaving in peaceful, studious, patient or courteous manners and so forth. By following these strategies when your child is "making you proud," you'll heap on positive energy when you see positive behaviors, values and character on display. Don't simply walk past a well behaved child and bypass an opportunity to share their greatness. Make eye contact, provide recognition, and then go. Allow the child to reap a benefit for doing what he's doing right or well.

A Success Story

My very good friend and fellow Advanced Trainer, Katherine Teasdale Edwards, shared the following story. I hope it inspires you.

Katherine said, "For reasons that aren't always clear to me in the moment — perhaps how I believe my children 'should' act or because I was feeling overwhelmed by the grind of my daily routine, or both — I found myself being a nagging and sometimes angry parent despite my optimistic, spiritually-focused outlook on life. The Nurtured Heart parenting approach offers a comprehensive way of interacting with my children, and others, that provides a language for me to verbalize their innate qualities of greatness and respond to them. My intention is to create inner wealth (love, kindness, confidence, joyousness) in my girls by affirming all of their wonderful ways of interacting with each other and the world. And when I fall back into my old, ineffective ways of interacting with my children, I acknowledge that is not what I want to be, dust myself off, and know that the next moment is a new moment for me to be the parent I aspire to be. That is the true gift of parenting in this fashion."

Stay in the moment with all recognitions; dust off if you make a mistake or your child makes a mistake. It's okay. Every new moment is just that — a new moment to begin anew. Nobody's perfect; and that isn't the goal!

Katherine used the Nurtured Heart Approach™ to teach toilet training to her youngest daughter, Hailey. Katherine said, "Using the approach to potty train? Is that over the top or what? No! It's the perfect example of how to use recognitions. Some parents get stuck while potty training and take their frustration out on the little one. Out of frustration from weeks of potty training, an accident might trigger 'How could you have that accident? I just asked you if you had to go and you said no!' I would have done the same. But my perspective was totally different this time around with my second daughter because of the approach. Obviously, as with many parents, there was lots of clapping and cheers when my daughter Hailey went to the bathroom on the potty. 'Hailey went potty, Hailey went potty' was accompanied by dancing on my part. Along with 'You are so independent and responsible for making it to the potty' and 'Look! You're going pee-pee on the potty.' When she did have accidents, either out and about or at home, we simply and swiftly changed her into new underwear and moved on. There was no focus on the accidents and lots of energy on the successes. Even the 'smaller' actions of our children's lives allow us to show them how great they really are. By switching our perspective and focusing all of our energy on Hailey having successful 'potty experiences' she was completely toilet trained so much quicker than it would otherwise have taken."

My friend Katherine is an Advanced Trainer of the approach and a blessing to me and so many others because of her calm, wise, kind and loving demeanor. Katherine uses the approach in her life and shares the greatness within her and others wherever she goes. Her two daughters, Holly and Hailey, are two beautiful children filled with inner wealth, inner strength, gloriousness, godliness and greatness because their mom is a woman who intends to congratulate and water the intrinsic greatness that already exists in them.

Children Love to Use the Language and Strategies, Too!

When you employ *Parenting Challenging Children with Power, Love and Sound Mind: The Nurtured Heart Approach™ from a Biblical Viewpoint* with a difficult child, your compliant children will likely beg you to tell them how wonderfully they're behaving, too! They'll want you to nurture and energize them with similar scrumptious language that marinates them in their own beautiful soul; they, too, will want to sow the same care and attention in others. You'll begin to hear your children use descriptive language on soccer fields, expressing how truly athletic and coordinated a teammate is. Your heart will melt with joy and warmth as you pay attention to your teenager telling her friend over the phone how impressed she is with her newfound skills in perception and insight. Children who had a hard time making friends will now be flooded with play dates and birthday invitations. Why? Because people *of all ages* want to be celebrated, not just tolerated!

Today my daughter Savannah forgot to take her lunch check to school. She called from school to ask if I would take it to her. Of course, I said yes.

When Savannah arrived home from school she immediately said, "Mom, thank you for bringing my lunch money to school today. You could have chosen not to bring it, but you displayed kindness and helpfulness. You are great!"

My son Chandler also cultivated some inner wealth in me today. After I pulled out of the driveway headed to an appointment, I had to call home because I forgot to tell my husband something. Chandler answered the phone and called to his dad. He was asked to tell me to hold because Brian was involved in a project. While waiting, Chandler came back on the phone and said, "Wow, Mom! You're being very patient and waiting well. I accuse you of being great today!"

Teach your children these strategies! Reap the benefits of raising children who take ordinary moments and turn them into opportunities to share with you how extraordinary many of your own choices are! It feels marvelous!

Put the Techniques into Action Now

You haven't been introduced yet to the limits and consequences parts of *Parenting with Power, Love and Sound Mind*. That happens in a subsequent chapter. Thank you for your patience and hard work up to this point. You've taken in a lot of information and are making great changes in your family. For now, work on keeping your thoughts focused on hope and on the positive use of your parental energy. Use recognitions liberally and concentrate on not giving any energy to negativity. Making these changes will certainly begin to impact your current family situation. You should be seeing less defiance and more compliance. Before, you may have intervened in a reactionary manner. Now you're being proactive, so discipline mode should be diminishing. But since you're dealing with children, you should expect times of disobedience and testing. For now, whenever that happens, simply remove all positive and negative energy from your interactions with your child, proclaim a "reset" or "time-out," and then, just moments later, bring your energy back to them and get them back in the game of displaying their greatness.

You Can Recognize Anything!

If you're thinking that recognizing your child's greatness will be a mind-blowing challenge, watch for ordinary and expected moments of life and then simply recognize the skills involved in addressing them.

For example, when you ask your children to put their dishes in the dishwasher, recognize that your child must:

- hear and listen to you;
- get up from his chair;
- push the chair in;
- walk to the dishwasher;
- neatly place the dish in the dishwasher;
- close the dishwasher.

The act required dexterity, coordination, and responsible behavior and a desire to please and obey you.

Another example: You ask your son to brush his teeth. In order to comply, he has to:

- listen and obey;
- get to the bathroom;
- turn on the light;
- get the toothbrush;

- put just the right amount of toothpaste on it;
- brush his teeth;
- turn the water on and off at appropriate times;
- clean the toothbrush;
- rinse his mouth and wipe his face;
- turn out the bathroom light.

These actions show your child displaying good listening skills, wise judgment, care of his body and health, respect for the conservation of energy, and a desire to keep a clean bathroom and toothbrush.

Remember the Four Guidelines and Stand Strong

Use your fellowship, liveliness and relational skills with your child to create transformation!

Purposefully move your child into success!

Refuse to strengthen negativity!

In the next chapter, we'll look at putting the final stand in place:
Courageously, fearlessly and relentlessly impose limits and consequences on your child!

Chapter Summary

Always give your children firsthand experiences in their world. Certain books, movies and examples may help a child learn, but educating in the moment as your child is displaying appropriate behaviors always works best. Throughout the day, provide lots of Active Recognitions, Experiential Recognitions, Proactive Recognitions and Creative Recognitions. Be strong in enforcing the four guiding principles and move from glory to glory with your child or teen. Look closely at ordinary moments to share all the beauty and great behaviors occurring in the moment. Memorize and hold strong to the principles you've learned in this book.

Questions for Reflection

1. What opportunities can I use to Actively Recognize my child and others around me at home, at work, within the community? Challenge yourself to Actively Recognize everyone you encounter. What opportunities have you missed to Actively Recognize someone?

2. What are the values and character qualities you want your child to internalize and display? Think back on times when you noticed your child displaying these values and you didn't comment. Next to each situation, what you could have said.

3. Proactive Recognitions recognize when rules are NOT being broken. List specific times in the past when you could have shared with your children that they were NOT breaking a rule. Today, start giving your children Proactive Recognitions and watch their reactions. How does it feel? How does it change the way your family interacts?

4. Creative Recognitions create irrefutable success by providing a request when the act is already in progress, or in a way that shows compliance is clear and needed. How did you make requests of your child in the past? What was the result? In what areas can you begin tapping into Creative Recognitions? Keep a journal of successes.

5. Count the number of times you recognize your child. The goal is to recognize your child 30 times a day for ten seconds each. Keep the journal to show your successes and improvements. Share the strategy and results with others.

Prayer for Today

Father, help me to Actively Recognize, Experientially Recognize, Proactively Recognize and Creatively Recognize my child. Give me the ability to recognize my child's feelings, to teach, name and allow my children healthy expression of feelings. Help me to find words to use that describe to my child the values and characteristics that are pleasing to You. Help me to create fair, just and wise rules and to tap into my inventive nature to create requests for success. Direct my path, keep me diligent, and give me strength to try this new way of talking. I pray this in the Name of my Lord and Savior, Amen.

TRANSFORMING LIMIT SETTING, CONSEQUENCES AND STRUCTURE

In this section you will learn how to correct your children when they are breaking the rules. I'll show you the rationale behind godly discipline, its true meaning, and how to enforce the rules. We will review the key components of the Nurtured Heart Approach™ Model for this particular area and discuss the "new time out." The section ends with a discussion about The Nurtured Heart Approach™ Credit System; A system designed by Howard Glasser to help you provide structure and to ensure that you are communicating a variety of recognitions.

Chapter 10:
Love: The Motive for Discipline

"My son, do not despise the Lord's discipline and do not resent his rebuke, because the Lord disciplines those he loves, as a father the son he delights in." (Proverbs 3:11)

The general points on discipline that will be emphasized throughout this chapter are: Love Is Essential, Keep It Centered, Don't Discipline in Anger and Rely on God.

Love is Essential

"Train-up a child in the way he should go and he will not depart from it." (Proverbs 22:6)

As parents, we need to keep our hearts filled with love, to make sure our thoughts are only on what is lovely, noble and pure. We need to make sure our words demonstrate our thoughts accurately and that they teach, edify and correct people in loving ways.

We've already learned how to become better communicators, sharing verbally and non-verbally what we see in a way that creates successes from all that <u>is</u> and <u>is not</u> pleasing to us.

Now we'll learn how to put all of this into action when things are not going well with our children and we need to do something to get them back on track.

Definition of Discipline

From the dictionary: Training expected to produce a specific character or pattern of behavior, especially training that produces moral or mental improvement (www.freedictionary.com).

From the Latin: **DISCIPULUS:** pupil and **DESCERE:** to learn. The purpose of discipline is to teach good behavior and responsible choices. Discipline is an opportunity to teach. (www.kitchenstewardship.com)

From the Greek: **DISCIPLINE** = **Paideía** *(NT: 3809)* originates from the following cognates; this path comes from Strong's Concordance; NT:3809 paideia (pahee-di'-ah); *from NT:3811;* **tutorage**, i.e. **education or training**; by implication, **disciplinary correction**. It appears this Greek word involves punishment with the idea of training and education in mind; in other words, not just hitting to punish, but with the "deed" (goal) of "training" (educating) the child. Of course, as noted, the "child" extends to adults as children of God. (www.bibleanswerstand.org)

From the Hebrew: **DISCIPLINE** = OT: 4148 muwcar (moo-sawr') **Muwcar;** chastisement, punishment, correction, discipline, **instruction, self — control**. This masc. noun is derived from yacar (3256). **Essentially, it is a bond, a checking, restraint, i.e., correction which results in education.** (See Deut. 11:2ff. [cf. Deut. 4:35ff.]). The term is very frequent in Proverbs (e.g., Prov. 3:11). **Often it is oral not corporal discipline. REPROOF = OT: 8433 towkechah** (to-kay-khaw'); and towkachath (to-kakh'-ath); from OT: 3198; **chastisement; figuratively (by words) correction, refutation, proof (even in defense).** (www.bibleanswerstand.org)

The above definitions illustrate that Godly discipline is necessary for the purpose of teaching and training. God is clear that you must discipline, present as an authority figure and regulate the behaviors of your child or teen. However, God finds it acceptable to discipline, teach and train your child and teen with means other than corporal punishment. If you intend to parent using *Parenting Challenging Children with Power, Love and Sound Mind: The Nurtured Heart Approach™ from a Biblical Viewpoint* you will want to abandon corporal punishment. Under this model corporal punishment is another way for your challenging child or teen to engage in relationship with you in a negative light. The goal of this approach is to teach and train your child when things are going well and to disengage with her when things are not going well.

To illustrate, when Savannah was much younger, we went to parenting classes at church and read Christian parenting books endorsing corporal punishment-even for the more challenging child. I didn't meet with success following this advice. Quite frankly, the advice backfired and I felt like a failure as a parent and with God. Even though Savannah was corporally disciplined in love, without any anger present in us and with a discussion of what she did wrong, we wound up seeing more of the same behavior she had been punished for and she became aggressive. Matters escalated to a point where Savannah decided that every time someone disobeyed her, she would corporally discipline them! This was not good! Not only did we have more of what we didn't want, we suddenly had a challenging child who thought that corporal punishment was a gift to give everyone who didn't follow the rules. We quickly abandoned the method and have had no regrets.

The other issue I take with corporal punishment is that most Christian and secular experts say that it should only be used for a season with children between a certain age range, the ranges vary but many say between 18 months and 8 years of age; and only for behaviors that are considered serious. It's my professional and experiential opinion that the best disciplinary approaches ought to be used throughout a person's lifetime. What a disempowering feeling to know that when your child reaches a certain age, your discipline method is outgrown and you have to start fresh. It seems apparent to me that one would want to stick with the same method throughout their parenting career. In addition, although at times we parents feel that the behaviors being exhibited are serious, if you take a deep breath and a step back they really are just children behaving in folly. Some proper guidance and training will make all of the difference.

In my profession, I have found most physical punishment happens for three reasons. The first is fear. For example, when a young toddler runs toward the street, you run after them as fast as you can. You spank them lightly and say no. This may be justifiable but, if you think about it, the action is done out of fear and to leave a definite impression about a certain action more than it is done to teach.

A second reason for corporal punishment is frustration. A parent struggling with a limited toolbox of skills reaches for the paddle in a last-ditch effort to solve a problem.

The third reason is often utter exhaustion. Parents face many demands in this fast-paced and difficult world. Sometimes life can overwhelm the best of us and we lash out at our young ones out of sheer frustration.

God has called us to discipline, teach and correct our children. And although He does allow corporal punishment, I firmly believe He has given us enough in His Word to enable us to provide sound instruction and punishment without resorting to physical discipline.

Children and Teens are Human, Too

"Children, obey your parents in the Lord, for this is right. Honor your father and mother-which is the first commandment with a promise-that it may go well with you and that you may enjoy long life on the earth." (Ephesians 6:1-3)

Children need to hear your thoughts and direction in a clear, consistent and loving way. They need to do what you say the first time you say it. They need to do it with respect and to honor your authority over them.

Children also must be free to make mistakes and to have safe opportunities to learn from their slip-ups and blunders.

Go ahead, read the above paragraphs again and let them sink in.

And here's the best part: We can get our children to do all the things listed above by parenting with loads of love, by clarifying the limits and boundaries, and by consistently enforcing the rules.

Keep it Centered

God expects us to lead our children with barrels of love and confessions of this love and to discipline and train up healthy, law-abiding, faith-filled individuals. If we are too permissive, overindulgent and lacking in structure, we'll reap unrestrained children who walk around with a sense of entitlement. They will be deficient in the servant attitude, an attitude which is very much lacking — and needed — in today's world.

If we use too many rules and restrictions, it causes extremes in a child's life. He'll live with fearfulness as a prime motivator and his individuality will be squashed; everything will be about keeping the peace or pleasing the person who causes fear or imposes control on his life.

As parents, an important goal is to be in control without being either overly controlling or overly permissive.

Do Not Discipline in Anger, But in Love

"... Do not let the sun go down while you are still angry...."
(Ephesians 4:26-28)

The above verse doesn't equate anger with offense, but it does say not to allow anger to lead us to transgression. As parents, we must remain in control ourselves — of our mind, body and soul. Parents who speak or act in anger usually regret it as soon as they calm down.

When you find yourself angry with your child, "reset" the stinking thinking and move on to something more productive. This allows you to deal with the situation in a timely manner without over-reacting. Don't hold on to your child's mistake or disobedience any more, for any reason. When dealing with your child, be clear and honest. Children live in folly and will test your abilities. They will hurt you, but it's rarely intentional. They don't realize the impact they're having and don't know how much they upset and hurt you.

"Love is patient, love is kind. It does not envy, it does not boast, it is not proud. It is not rude, it is not self seeking, it is not easily angered, it keeps no record of wrongs. Love does not delight in evil but rejoices with the truth. It always protects, always trusts, always hopes, always perseveres. Love never fails....And now these remain: faith, hope and love. But the greatest of these is love."
(1 Corinthians 13:4-8,13)

Raising children is both a reward and a great responsibility. A child must know that he is unconditionally loved without limit before discipline will have the effect you want. Your goal is not to hurt or damage your children, but to guide them to become the adults God wants them to be. A relationship of care, concern, guidance, protection and general well-being must be in place for effective discipline to occur; otherwise (and you can take this to the bank) your child will rebel. It's your job to send your children into the world healthy and whole.

Rely on God

It is vital as we discipline our children to do so in a Godly manner. We must be guided by our spirit, not our emotions or flesh. This is especially true when we're battling intense emotions. When we rely on God, we rely on the Holy Spirit to be our guide.

Key Points of Discipline

1.) Always Present a United Front
2.) Create and Maintain Boundaries
3.) Teach Responsibility and Appropriate Behavior
4.) Just Say No
5.) You Must Be In Control

Always Present a United Front

Children are especially good at getting what they want. One way is to "divide and conquer" the parents!

Eleven year old Sarah Jean wanted to go to her friend's party. The party was for boys and girls in her class; the parents of the child hosting the party would be there.

Two of Sarah Jean's friends, with whom she was not allowed to hang out with because they were starting to get into trouble at school, would also be there. Sarah Jean knew that if she asked her mother, she would receive a "yes." Her mother understood that Sarah Jean could go to a party, behave responsibly, and not interact too much with bad influences.

But dear old Dad? Sarah Jean wasn't going to ask his permission to attend the party because she knew the answer would be a resounding "No way! You're too young to go to a party. End of discussion."

So Sarah Jean marched into Mom's room to ask if she could go to the party. As predicted, her mom said yes. Dad walked in at that moment, overheard the conversation, and informed both of them that a party for an eleven-year-old was an unwise decision. Mom and Dad spent the evening arguing and Sarah Jean got a ride to the party with the next door neighbor.

That's how it happens. Sarah Jean knew who to ask and exactly what it would take to get the spotlight off her request.

Parental control is always the loser in the divide-and-conquer game. It's important to discuss parenting issues in private, and to offer a united front ALL THE TIME, even when you don't agree on a particular matter. As soon as you create dissension in front of your children, it becomes a ticket to ride, their own way, any time they want it.

Children test the waters before they jump in. They'll test you and explore; it's part and parcel of their nature. In 2 Timothy 3:2 Paul points out that children will be disobedient to their parents. As trying as it is at times to deal with the same issue over and over, your children are just doing what comes naturally. Children are natural boundary testers. It's in their job description to if you're looking, to see how far they can push you, and what the best outcome will be.

Create and Maintain Boundaries

"For God is not a God of disorder but of peace."
(1 Corinthians 14:33)

It's in our parental job description to give our children boundaries which are safe, secure and non-negotiable.

Four-year-old Shawn was the quintessential boundary tester. His parents Jonathon and Amanda, took him out for a nice family day together. Shawn first tried to walk without holding hands in the park. He boldly and defiantly declared that he was a big boy and didn't need to hold hands.

After that scuffle, which repeated ten times, they entered the park, in which Shawn tried to run up to people's dogs to pet them. He had to be sequestered at the picnic area at least three times for this offense.

Shawn refused to eat his lunch but wanted his dad to buy him a soda and an ice cream from a vendor because he was hungry for that kind of food. Finally, when it was time to go, Shawn needed just five more minutes on the swings. Ten minutes later Shawn still needed five more minutes.

You place boundaries for good reasons: to teach obedience and to keep your children safe. Boundaries must be enforced, and enforced swiftly, without hesitation or hiccup. The rules are the rules; that's the rule!

The moment a child gets the sense that a boundary can be moved when severely tested, trouble lies ahead. When she knows she can test it until the cows come home and she will still not get what she wants, she will, by her own choice, back off and learn that it just isn't worth it to keep on trying for something that will yield no reward as a result of her perseverance.

Jonathon and Amanda don't sweat their little boundary tester anymore. Shawn is now six and doing just fine. He knows where the line is. Jonathon and Amanda give him loads of love for following the plan and when he has moments of testing they simply "reset" him, put him back into the right flow, and move on.

"Folly is bound up in the heart of a child, but the rod of discipline will drive it far from him." (Proverbs 22:15)

Children are works in progress. They will, on occasion, be foolish.

When my husband and I purchased an old farmhouse, it took an entire year to work out the boundary issues. Our house was being separated from a large farm. We were only buying two acres of land with the farmhouse. The boundaries, or line of demarcation, had to be clearly surveyed and recorded so we could legally have the piece of property we agreed to purchase.

Boundaries are essential ingredients for proper parenting, too. Children who have fuzzy, non-existent or inconsistent boundaries end up confused, angry, spoiled and a host of other negative things. Without knowledge of good, there can be no understanding of evil. When we accept a job, we know our duties, our hours and all the stipulations required to do it correctly. In other words, boundaries are important in every area of life. We need them to navigate successfully. There are no exceptions for children.

Boundaries enable peaceful co-existence. If everyone knows the rules and follows the rules, peace and joy abound. Boundaries provide a foundation and define when a rule is broken and requires restoration. Boundaries provide security. They let a child know what's going to happen from morning to night so they don't have to worry or wonder. Boundaries help build responsibility. As a child grows and matures, the boundary lines can be moved as trust is earned and extended.

Boundaries bring success to children because they form the world in which the child lives. Boundaries need to be well understood and based on the Word of God and the welfare of the family. As such, boundaries bring blessings to all who follow them. Boundaries must be clear, consistent and fair. It's also wise to set boundaries only in the areas in which you are willing and able to enforce them.

Teach Responsibility and Appropriate Behavior

As parents, it's our job to teach children to put folly aside as they grow. This isn't to say we're to teach our children to stop having fun. Instead, we need to teach our children to behave responsibly and appropriately in all situations, even (and especially) when they're having fun.

Sixteen-year-old JoAnna and her friends loved to go joy-riding during the hot summer months. During one of their nighttime adventures, JoAnna and her friends thought it would be "funny" to bring a tool kit and take down a few street signs. One sign she took down had her last name on it. JoAnna proudly brought the sign home and put it up in her room to show off her trophy.

Brandon, Miles, Scott and Tucker all thought it would be "totally awesome" to go down to the local bridge and jump into the water below. The "DANGER! No Swimming" signs that jutted from the sharp, rocky riverbank were ignored because the boys were all good swimmers.

It's our job to teach our children obedience, right and wrong, safe and unsafe, to instill in them the best possible judgment for the times when they will be making potentially life-changing decisions.

Just Say No

A manipulator can really mess up a parent. Manipulators know right where to hit the heart of an unsuspecting mommy or daddy and come out victorious! Manipulators are skilled craftsman in the art of pouty faces, puffed-out lips, cutesy behavior and tear-shedding.

Charise is a six-year-old master of the ruse. When Charise wants something and is told no, she can tilt her head down and peek up at you with giant brown eyes that look like warm, just-out-of-the-oven brownies. Charise has mastered the technique of getting what she wants by saying, doing or looking a certain way.

How do you stop a weapon of mass destruction like Charise? You don't fall for it. Sometimes we have to stay strong and know in our gut that the "no" we hear ourselves saying is the right word. Trust me: "No" really is the perfect response sometimes! I promise her life will not be over, even if she tells you it will be. I can assure you she will not be the ONLY kid who doesn't have a new pair of hundred dollar shoes.

You — In Control!

Parents correct children. Children do not correct parents. A parent is in control. A child is not in control. Never allow the lines to blur when working with authority. Children are to respect and obey their parents.

The Role of Parents

Know What's Going On At All Times

Parents need to know every detail of their children's lives to ensure they're on a proper path. Shepherds are a fabulous example of this. Shepherds know the state of their flocks at all times and know everything there is to know about each sheep.

> *"I am the good shepherd; I know my sheep and my sheep know me."*
> *(John 10:14)*

Know who your children spend time with, know where they're going and coming from, know what they like and don't like. You can never know too much about the child God has given you to raise!

Remain Teachable and Seek Help When You Need It

> *"For lack of guidance a nation falls, but many advisers make a victory sure." (Proverbs 11:14)*

The minute we think we know everything there is to know, we're in trouble. Check out the world your children live in. Know about their Facebook, Twitter, and MySpace pages and the internet in general. Stay current with your children. Show them you're intensely interested in whatever interests them. Unless they're doing something unsavory, they'll love your involvement! When you don't know something or can't find it out, seek sound advice from a counselor, pastor, teacher, coach, close friend or mentor. When you need help, reach out and get it. When you do, you're revealing empowerment, not weakness.

Provide Wise Counsel to Your Children

Children value the advice of the people they trust and love. Proverbs 19:20 says, *"Listen to advice and accept instruction, and in the end you will be wise."* When you share with your children in a non-judgmental, non-critical way how you would handle something, or when you help them to discern an answer or a way forward, you're providing them with counsel.

Be a Role Model

"In everything set them an example by doing what is good."
(Titus 2:7)

Teaching your children how to behave by simply "doing likewise" will do wonders.

- If you want your children to be responsible, show them what being responsible looks like: model responsible behavior.
- If you want your children to be neat, clean your house, do your laundry and dress neatly.
- If you want them to be good with money, show them you tithe, offer and have savings and investment accounts. Show them that you only spend what the budget allows.

By teaching your children the various ways in which you engage with the world, you instill in them an ability to manage intense emotions and serious issues with faith, a proper attitude and grace.

Have a Life Outside of Your Children

Yep, I said it! Not only is it okay but, at times, it's *imperative* to leave your children at home with a babysitter while you recharge or reconnect with your spouse. It's perfectly fine for you to have hobbies, interests and talents that don't include your children. Remember, your children are on loan from God. You're to bring them up and move them out. You need to have a life outside of your children, too. Interests outside your children help fulfill your multi-faceted nature and keep you in touch with friends and other things that only adults can appreciate and enjoy.

Teach Children about Jesus

"These commandments that I give you today are to be upon your hearts. Impress them on your children. Talk about them when you sit at home and when you walk along the road, when you lie down and when you get up." (Deuteronomy 6:6-7)

As parents, we're responsible to bring to Jesus all of our children under the age of thirteen. If you're married, both parents should agree on what bringing your children to faith will look like. If you're single, you're taking on the role of mother and father in the arena of discipline. What you say will go. For divorced or separated parents, do the best you can based on God's word and have faith that God is in control. Apply with great determination all of the principles you've learned and trust that what you're instilling in your children will be carried on in their hearts whenever they're away from you.

Forgiveness as Part of Discipline

"Who is a God like you, who pardons sin and forgives the transgressions of the remnant of his inheritance? You do not stay angry forever but delight to show mercy, you will again have compassion on us; you will tread our sins underfoot and hurl all our iniquities into the depths of the sea."
(Micah 7:18-19)

Parenting with Power, Love and Sound Mind will not be complete unless you offer up forgiveness to your child or teen every time restoration is needed. When working with the concept of forgiveness, there are three main components: receive forgiveness from God through Jesus Christ for your wrongdoings; forgive yourself for every mistake you have ever made; forgive others so you can walk in the peace, joy and rest that come from God. Follow these three rules yourself and teach them to your child or teen. How awesome the world would be if we <u>all</u> walked in love and forgiveness <u>all</u> of the time.

How Discipline Fits in with Parenting with Power, Love and Sound Mind

In *Parenting with Power, Love and Sound Mind* you're learning a method of discipline that is consistent with Scripture. You'll parent with relentless courage by giving a consequence (discipline) for disobedient acts without the need for corporal punishment. I've used this approach in my own home and taught it to countless others. I can state without equivocation that this approach encapsulates the instruction of the Lord in such a way that inner wealth, inner strength, gloriousness, godliness and greatness of the child springs forth like water from an artesian well.

Chapter Summary

In this chapter, we've been reminded that we're commanded to discipline our children. The goal of discipline is to train and teach our children and teens so they become responsible individuals who are able to make wise choices. Children have the job of testing us and making mistakes so they can learn and grow. As parents we have the job of providing boundaries, acting as united fronts, teaching responsible and appropriate behavior and just saying no. We are to behave as role models, have interests outside of our children, know what is going on at all times, seek wise counsel when necessary and share our faith with our children.

Questions and Points for Reflection

1. Identify and explore your own beliefs about discipline and punishment. Share in a journal or with someone close to you.
2. Ask yourself how your beliefs surrounding discipline help or hinder your goals and intentions for your children.
3. Are you providing discipline and consequences in a manner God would find pleasing?
4. Create a list of areas for you to consider in setting boundaries. Some examples may be: play, chores, school, eating, hygiene, prayer and worship, bedtime and friends.
5. What are some interests you have other than your child or teen?
6. Who are some of your role models and wise counselors?

Prayer

Father God, thank You that You are a God of discipline, love, forgiveness, grace and mercy. Please help me to discipline my challenging child or teen in a manner that is acceptable and pleasing to You. Help me to provide them all the structure, boundaries, rules and limits that will help them to excel. Show me ways in which I can be a more involved parent that is consistent with sharing my power and authority in healthy ways. Give me the strength to rear my children or teens with the kind of teaching and training that will last a lifetime and bring them from glory to glory. I pray this in the Name of Jesus, Amen.

Chapter 11:
Train Up a Child:
Effective Limit Setting
and Consequences

"I have missed more than 9000 shots in my career. I have lost almost 300 games. On 26 occasions I have been entrusted to take the game-winning shot... and missed. And I have failed over and over and over again in my life. And that is why I succeed." (Michael Jordan)

In the previous chapter we learned that God wants us to impose discipline in love, which simply means to teach and train our children and teens. In this chapter, we'll learn how to implement specific strategies of correction straight from the Nurtured Heart Approach™ model. Before we begin, I must tell you that the most effective defense against poor behavior is offense. The more light you shed on your child's or teen's successes, the more those will begin to appear and the less you will need to discipline.

Effective limit-setting and consequences are based on the principal of reset, restore and recover. God created this world and placed boundaries everywhere we look. The water, sky and earth all have limitations and dividing lines. The Ten Commandments and all the other rules in the Bible provide us with boundaries, rules and limits. When we break a rule or cross a boundary, we're given a consequence. As soon as we see our error we can ask for forgiveness and receive the limitless grace and mercy of God, through Jesus Christ, and receive the forgiveness that places us immediately back into fellowship with God. In the same way, when our children do wrong, it is our job to reset them, take them out of fellowship with us, forgive them as soon as we see the first signs of repentance and allow them to recover by coming back into relationship with us.

The Referee's Rule Book: Parents, Rule Like a Referee

All sports have rules and the people who play them know every single one of them. They don't need the rules explained every time they set foot on the playing surface. In fact, everyone involved with a sport, including the referees, spectators and commentators are acquainted with the rules and how they relate to the court or field being played on.

Take basketball, for example. When a player steps out of bounds with the ball, the referee blows his whistle and unceremoniously declares a rule was broken. The game stops for a second while everyone readjusts, the appropriate consequence for the infraction is imposed, and the game begins again. The neutral, unceremonious referee quickly indicates that an infraction has occurred by blowing a whistle. He doesn't stop the game to lecture, humiliate, abuse, nag or yell at the player. No discussion occurs, the consequence is served, and the player is back in the game.

This is how Parenting with Power, Love and Sound Mind works too. All of the relational power is about being in the game and playing the game right. When an infraction occurs, the game stops briefly, no more delicious liveliness is flowing, the consequence is perceived or felt, and the game begins anew. More time and energy are spent in the game than out of it.

Before moving on, let's look at a couple more things. First, consider the referee: a good referee or official is neutral. He isn't on any side and is there simply to ensure that the rules are enforced. The referee is expected to stay calm, provide accurate accounts of a situation, and give fair consequences for an action. When infractions occur in your home, stay calm, remain neutral, be fair with the consequences, and ensure that you've made an accurate call.

Second, at a competitive sporting event the rules and boundaries are clear and simple and everyone knows them. This provides structure, safety and a successful game. The rules aren't fuzzy and ever-changing and the boundary lines remain solidly in their places throughout the game.

Let's take this strategy into a kindergarten room. If I were to tell a kindergartner to be respectful, how would she understand what I was saying? She would either have no idea what I meant, or she would discern from her experiences at home what respect might mean — which is purely subjective to each family — or she'll pretend to know but not really get it. Any of these assumptions on her part could get her into hot water at school. But what if, instead of saying "Be respectful" I say, "No hitting" or

"No talking when someone else is talking." Our little tyke will understand immediately what her boundaries are.

The Bottom Line: Rules Must Be Clear, Simple and Start with No

Rules that start with *"NO"* make sense; they point out a boundary where one may not have existed before. This makes everyone's life much easier. Life makes sense. Our children don't arrive knowing what to do or how to behave. It's our job to teach them how to behave. Rules that are clear, simple and start with *"NO"* make your job much easier.

Rules Should Start with No for clarity and structure

No hitting
No teasing
No spitting
No foul language
No dirty laundry on the floor
No talking when someone else is talking

Crystal-clear rules set up a perfect structure and boundaries and allow additional opportunities to give kudos for success by appreciating the things that are going well.

Establish an appreciation for the times when destructive behaviors are not happening. When children make a mistake, they serve their consequence without fanfare and then are ushered back into relationship with you with the message, "You did the time-out very well. Now get back in the game."

Your Child Already Knows the Rules

Your children know the rules unless they're infants. You can create a list, you can have calm discussion about it, but believe me, they already know when they cross a line. I've asked hundreds of kids of all ages if they know when they're breaking a rule and everyone has said, "Yes."

I was watching "Little People, Big World" the other day. The show documents the lives of a Christian family, some of whom are Little People.

The episode I caught showed the mother and father going off to Hawaii and leaving the children home alone. The mother compiled and recited a list of rules to the kids. After they left, one of the boys said he didn't know why his mom needed to read the rules to them. They all knew them.

Deliver Time-Outs Unceremoniously and Without Emotional Expression

This is a crucial key: When your children break a rule, unceremoniously and in a neutral tone tell them, "Oops! broke a rule" or "reset," "time-out," "take a break," "red light" or any other word or phrase with which you're comfortable that will remove your power (attention) from them. Wait for them to pull themselves together and get back under control (hang tight...I will show you what to do when a child will not reset quickly on their own) and immediately acknowledge when the "reset" is successful and get them back in the game with verbal and non-verbal appreciation.

This may be the most difficult concept to understand. The amount of time you spend on the "wrong" should be minimized to a simple, unemotional acknowledgement of the wrong and a "reset."

A time-out is the sole consequence for any broken rule. Never engage in any discussion, explanation or sermon. Simply deliver the consequence each and every time a rule is broken.

Typical parenting strategies have a punitive feeling to them, a sense that the "punishment must fit the crime" or the child won't learn the lesson. The traditional mindset doesn't work as well as this Approach does. You need the mind of Jesus to be an exceptional parent. Jesus practiced forgiveness of sins, mercy and grace. When your child makes a mistake or misbehaves, he'll receive a momentary lapse of relationship (which we call the reset) and an interruption of the problem, and as soon as the reset is over, he'll receive forgiveness and move back into deep and intimate relationship with you again. *It should never be the punishment that gets your child's attention; it should be your positive power, energy and enthusiasm upon welcoming him back into relationship with you that becomes the payoff.* Take away your relational presence whenever a child expresses negative behaviors and heap it on during times of success. This method pays valuable dividends.

Consistency is Key

You will no longer warn, lecture, nag, yell, scream or spank to get your children to comply. You also will no longer look the other way, no matter how benevolent or transcendental you may be feeling on any given day. Just as our referee in the example above is expected to call out EVERY offense, you must do it, too. That means you'll need to be consistent. Looking the other way or forgiving from time to time without a reset confuses the child and blurs the line. Consistency is absolutely vital.

When you were in high school, did you have hall monitors? I did. I knew which ones were strict, which ones would let me get away with things, and which ones couldn't be trusted. Consistency was key.

But suppose you have the same hall monitor every day. Let's call her Mom. One day she's in a good mood, so she lets you walk by with your hat on, even though hats are not allowed in school. The next day, you walk by with your hat on, thinking it will be all right, but Mom didn't sleep well, has a headache and is in a bit of a snit. Today she snaps at you and tells you to get the hat off now or she will write you up. You don't understand and are feeling a bit hurt and angry and really confused and frustrated because that isn't how Mom reacted to your hat yesterday. Finally, on the third day you walk by Mom with your hat on again and today she doesn't even seem to notice you, except to glance your way and frown a little. So what's your impression of this lady after three days? You just keep going, all the while thinking to yourself, "This lady is nuts!"

Sad to say, this kind of thing happens all the time in our homes at varying times and degrees. When we aren't consistent, our children spend time wondering about boundaries and testing us to determine where the boundary is on a given day. Make the rules and enforce them. Consistency saves you from this mistake.

Avoid Using Warnings

A warning gives power to a negative situation. If you say things like, "If you do that again, I'll…," or "I've had a rough day, so please don't fight with your brother," you're leaking negativity. Warnings send negative messages to a child's portfolio and give relationship to negative situations. Instead of

"Please stop fighting," use "Reset," wait a few seconds until you see a change in attitude, then say, "Thanks for putting yourself back in the game. Right now you're being calm, respectful and kind."

Warnings can do more damage than creating negative energy, which is damaging enough. Warnings blur boundaries. If a child is given inconsistent boundaries and structure, you create a world where constant testing can take place. Your child will wonder at every turn, "I wonder what will happen if I do this today?" And since the answer or consequence is generally different from day to day depending on your mood, your child receives a different response every time. Inconsistency, lack of structure and boundaries confuse and propel a child out of control. Continual testing and rule breaking becomes the behavior of choice.

Warnings also communicate a lack of trust. Constant repetition of rules and warnings teach children we don't trust them enough to know the rules. Allow them the firsthand experience of breaking a rule so they can learn there is no benefit to breaking it again and that they receive more relationship, success and accolades for following the rules than for breaking them.

"Time-In" Versus "Time-Out"

Consequences of any kind are "time-outs" from life's enjoyable activities. When you corrected your children using traditional methods, you perhaps had them sit in the "naughty chair," sent them to bed, took away the car, "grounded" them, took the cell phone, or removed video games. These are all times when your child was no longer in the game for a specified period of time. She was disconnected from the life she wanted to pursue, and from you. When you contaminate a time-out with lectures, warnings, ("I'm sorry to have to do this to you," "This hurts me more than it hurts you,") or anything else, you reward negativity by giving your relationship to it. When you correct the *Parenting with Power, Love and Sound Mind* way, your child will get no positive or negative attention from you during the time-out because you won't reward the poor choice they have made. Make sense?

Time-Out To-Do List

1. Create a term for your family to use to specify a time-out is occurring. It can be "time-out," "take a break," "reset" or any other term you choose.

2. Give a zero energy, neutral, unceremonious "time-out" EVERY time an infraction occurs and a rule is broken.

3. Give absolutely NO energy during this time: No discussion, no talking, no non-verbal cues that you're upset. Stay cool and silent no matter what!

4. Make the time-out quick and simple.

5. As soon as the consequence is over, invigorate success and make time in better than being in time-out.

It's confusing to children to receive negative relationship. If you're yelling, screaming or lecturing during a time when the child should receive no energy at all because of a bad choice, the child realizes he is getting lots of attention and energy from you (think "favorite toy") when he's misbehaving and you just lose the point of the reset entirely. Correcting a child the old-fashioned way keeps them in the game (energy and interaction-wise) when they should be out of it. Consequence: you'll get more of the behavior you want to eliminate. Basically, you become your own worst enemy when you warn, nag, lecture, scream, yell, threaten, etc.

"Time-out" should always be an absolute disconnect from any form of relationship, positive or negative liveliness, or anything else that brings pleasure, relationship, energy or attention to the child. "Time-in" is everything else. "Time-in" allows the flow of positive relational energy and the positive feelings of being connected to you, and it allows the child to do what she enjoys. During "time-in," children are in the loop, living life with success. ***Simply put, if your children are not in "time-out" they are in "time-in."***

Keep Time-Outs Brief

When you put your children in time-out, you're taking them out of the game and taking away their sense of connection to you and the world around them. time-out should be short — just seconds or a few minutes long. Quick time-outs set children back on track, and help both the children and parents move on to the next moment of opportunity for success. Best of all, time-outs can be done anywhere.

Quickie time-outs can be given at a store, where the child is standing, on the couch — the place of restriction no longer matters. What matters is that he feels a consequence for inappropriate behavior and the goal becomes getting back in control of himself so he can get back in the game. With younger children, it's fine — and may be preferable — to have a designated place for the time-out, but again, it isn't necessary. One technique that may help is turning your back or walking away from the misbehaving child along with a neutral, "That's a time-out." If you do this, be sure to clearly state the action that put them into a time-out because very young children often don't have a clue that something they do may be inappropriate, dangerous, or wrong.

With this approach, time-outs don't need to last the traditional one-minute-per-age of the child. Your goal is to get your child to feel a disruption of relational power when she misbehaves and allow a shift in behavior to occur. Under these circumstances, a time-out begins as soon as your child "freezes" like a statue or simply becomes quiet or adopts a calm demeanor. As soon as this happens, the time-out should end and an energy-filled fiesta should ensue; welcome your child back into loving relationship with you, a joyous occasion for both. So time-out can be as long as it takes to turn your back, or for the child to become quiet and stop moving and talking. A time-out of 10 to 15 seconds will work and be effective, too. *As the parent, you are in control of the time-out, so you decide when the time-out is over. Your child doesn't get a vote on the duration of the time-out, ever.* Needless to say, don't forget to end the reset and put them back into the game!

When You Feel a Sermon Coming On

Use Proactive Recognition times to deliver sermons or lectures to your child. Please recall that Proactive Recognition occurs with children ONLY during times they're not breaking a rule. So, when your child has served his time-out and you allow him back into the game, bring him back by "accusing" him of not breaking the rules. Example: If Timmy was in time-out for throwing a toy, deliver the "sermon" after the child has recovered from the time-out and is being successful, then say, "Timmy, you're not throwing toys right now. That shows you know how to follow the rules. You're doing great!"

Time-Outs Transform

Time-outs help you and your child. When you guide with a time-out mentality, you show your child that you can handle intense situations and emotions in a healthy manner, too, so you're modeling appropriate behavior during these times. Time-outs also send the message that your child can handle intense emotions, too, and that you trust that they can handle them. The time-out strategy also encourages children, because it's quick and they don't ever live in fear, guilt or shame. On the flip side you, too, are free to enjoy your child more often and leave behind the discomfort of having to lower her self-esteem whenever she makes a bad choice.

The Hockey Game: One More Way to Parent Like a Referee

Parents and teachers alike have an "AHA!" moment whenever I teach them the analogy of the hockey game.

I spent my first year in college in Northern New York, very near the Canadian border where the weather was usually freezing or very cold. Because of this, athletic people in the area pursued and enjoyed winter sports. Almost everyone watches or plays hockey in the North Country. Hockey is an intense sport that requires great skill. You need to maneuver quickly and deftly on the ice, carry a stick, and slam a puck into a goal.

Occasionally, hockey players will do something inappropriate and be sent to the penalty box. The referee will blow the whistle, usher the player to the box, and specify the amount of time-out for the offense. The player goes to the box sits, usually on the edge of his seat, watching as the game goes on without him.

All the excitement is on the ice. The player in the box wants out of the box and back onto the ice in the worst way. He gets no reward or thrill sitting in the box — he's alone and out of the game. When the buzzer sounds to end the penalty phase, the player flies out of the penalty box and back onto the ice with tremendous anticipation and enthusiasm.

As a parent, consider yourself the referee at a hockey game. You make calls and send your errant child to the penalty box. The penalty box is a place of silence next to an energized, zest-filled game. The box is the reset and the game is the energy you zing your child with the moment he leaves the penalty box and is once again behaving appropriately. The penalty box is not to punish, it is merely to help teach and train your child take a breath and reorganize his choices to get back into the game.

Common Scenarios:

What to do when Your Child Blows Up or Threatens You

If your child calls you stupid, says she hates you, throws something, or behaves in some other way that's offensive, allow yourself to feel your own feelings. If you're angry, frustrated and worn out, go ahead and feel what you're feeling, but then move on. Don't give in to arguments, lectures, sermons, negotiations, crying, swearing, chasing or discussing. Simply say, "The reset will begin when you're quiet and standing still." Calmly repeat the direction even if your child talks back or yells at you. If you must say something, use Experiential Recognition, "Yikes! I see you're very intense right now and are trying to find words to help express yourself. Great honesty." "I am confident that you are strong enough to calm yourself down."

Time-Out Tip

In the beginning, it may take many "resets" before compliance happens. Don't lose hope and stick with the plan. It works!

When the time-out is over remember to lavish your child with the skills displayed for completing it. If a wrong has occurred, tell them to make it right. You may choose to say, *"You sat so well through that time-out. I appreciate that you were able to accept the consequences of breaking a rule, even though you were angry with me for deciding you needed one. That's a wonderful decision you made."* Remember, your child could have continued the misbehavior or escalated it. Acknowledge the positive truth of the moment. If you believe you need to address the behavior, do it proactively after the time-out is over and your child is back in the game. Acknowledge them during times when they're speaking respectfully and not throwing things; let them know how much you appreciate their respect and consideration.

Public Time-Outs

It can be hard to enforce a time-out in public. You may worry about what onlookers may think, say or do. Enforce time-outs anyway! If you don't, your child will get the message that she can get away with more when you're in public. Teach her you're serious about the approach and that you enforce it everywhere. Share the intentions you have for your child before entering the public place: *"Sweetheart, we're going into the store. You can walk next to me and look at the items in the store, but you are not allowed to touch them. I see you as a person of strength, with wonderful self-control."*

If a rule is broken, tell the child, "That's a time-out." Don't warn, scold, lecture or nag. Quickly, efficiently and clearly call a time-out. The time-out begins when your child is quiet and standing still. If your child refuses the time-out, explain that she will have a consequence when she gets home. Give no energy or expression to her refusal; simply move on. Remember to enforce the time-out when you get home.

Multiple Children, Same Kudos?

The same thing isn't always fair. Parents frequently think that giving the same thing to every one of their children is the right way to prove all are equally loved. This may be the case when buying Christmas presents but even then, sometimes it fails. If you buy two coloring books, one for each of your children, but one child doesn't like to color, you're not honoring or benefiting one of them.

While it's appropriate and I strongly encourage you to give the same number of recognitions to each of your children, be sure to honor each of them as the unique individuals they are. Praise them for their own strengths, talents, abilities and character development. Use different words and language to energize each child at his or her own level.

If one child misbehaves and another doesn't, share delicious relational cues with the one that behaves and give a time-out to the one that isn't. "Thomas, reset." "Sandra, you're petting the dog gently without pulling his tail. Thank you for following the rules and showing kindness to one of God's creatures." "Thomas, thank you for completing your time-out. You sat still when you really didn't want to. You're being obedient and displaying personal power. You're back in the game and can go back to playing kindly with the dog."

Siblings should be told to stay away from and not talk to or tease a sibling who is in time-out. A time-out needs to be a solitary event without any interference.

The Honeymoon Before the Explosion

Be prepared for your child's "honeymoon" when you launch the new approach. He may well bask in the glory of all the new love language and start out behaving like a superstar. Then, out of nowhere, will come the tsunami of all tests.

It happened with my children and I've heard similar stories from other parents. This is not to say all children and teens behave in this manner. I share this nugget of information in the event it happens at your house for the purpose of keeping you on track. Children react this way because they get used to the "dances" we do with them.

In my case, Chandler and I would do a "dance of negativity" every Saturday during chore time. Chandler and I both expected for him to refuse and avoid doing his chores and for me to nag, yell and threaten when he didn't do them.

One Saturday after learning the approach, chore time came but Chandler didn't know how to interpret the language. The approach worked everywhere else in our home for him, but our adversarial behavior was habitual with him. I stuck to the process. My intention was to handle the scene with the approach firmly in place.

As Chandler screamed at me, insulted me, threw things, dumped garbage on the floor and moved around the house in a fury, I calmly told him I knew he could handle his intense emotions and that I was confident he would be able to do a reset. Chandler didn't back down for 45 minutes and finally stomped up to his room, where he fell asleep for two hours. The poor thing was worn out from all of his energy expenditure! He returned after his nap and I thanked him for doing his reset. Chandler cried and apologized. I shared with him that we were on to the next success and the past was behind us. I also gave him his chore list and tacked on some reasonable community service. It has been years since that outburst and we've not had one like it again. In honor of Chandler, I need to share. Chandler has, on many occasions, been able to demonstrate mastery of handling intense emotions. He has a wildly wonderful sense of humor, a giant heart and a natural gift to nurture others.

Keep in mind that when children are new to something they will test, they will be confused with the new ways, and they will want the old ways back, even if they weren't healthy, because they're predictable. You need to teach your child that this new language, philosophy and approach are here to stay and that they can count on you to adhere to its boundaries.

Also keep in mind that children and teens are growing. They can be expected to have outbursts and issues as they grow and change. Modify the approach and the rules as they learn and develop new skills, levels of responsibility and trust.

When they refuse a Time-Out

When your child refuses to do a time-out; especially in the beginning when you're both learning, think back to the Toll Taker and Shamu strategies. The goal is for the child to experience the illusion that they're not going to receive vigor or relationship for undesirable behavior. Look for any moment, brief as it might be, where you see the child being still and when he is, say something like "Wow! Your time-out is over, and you did it even though you really didn't want to do it and were feeling angry. I see you making an effort to gain self control. You are responsible and filled with good judgment."

The goal of a time-out is not to punish the child but to give her an experience that takes her out of the game of life so she wants to get back into being successful again. Create the illusion of a time-out and allow her to breathe in accomplishment. Her next refusals will be fewer and farther in between.

Giving Time-Out to an Older Child or Teen

Time-outs work with older children and teens, too, but I don't recommend making them sit in a chair or a designated spot. The best thing to do with an older child or teen is to say, "That's a time-out" and move away or turn your body from them. As soon as there is quiet and your child approaches you with calmness, energize the success of completing the time-out. If he was given a time-out for not completing something, the best course of action is to share the success you see and then advise him to get to work on the chore or request. For severe or larger infractions, community service can be part of the time-out consequence.

Time-Out Tips

From *All Children Flourishing: Igniting the Greatness of Our Children* by Howard Glasser with Melissa Lynn Block (2007)

Don't escalate or energize when the child doesn't jump into time-out right away.	**Do** allow the child a few moments to accept and begin the time-out. Nagging or pressuring the child to start the time is tantamount to handing out $100 bills for poor choices.
Don't thank a child for completing the time-out without saying why you are appreciative. Then, rather than conveying that the child is doing you a favor; you are acknowledging that she has made a wise choice.	**Do** acknowledge the child's self-control and ability to redirect himself; or his maturity in accepting the consequences of his actions; or the good example he's setting for his siblings by quickly accepting his time-out and getting back on track.
Don't explain which rule has been broken.	**Do** trust that the child knows which rule has been broken. Keep a sharp eye out for demonstrations of that same rule being followed rather than broken, then reflect back to the child: "Jenny, I see that you're now choosing to sit peacefully in your chair and ear your dinner instead of teasing your sister. You are following the rules now and showing good focus and respect for others."
Don't be roped into a battle over whether time-out is needed, or react to any displays of bad attitude that arise in response to the time-out.	**Do** drain all of the energy, relationship, effort emotion and time from your responses to your child's negative reaction to a time-out. Remain unaffected by pleading, arguing, insults, tantrums and fussing engaged in by the child to try to get your features popping.

Don't add more time to the time-out in response to the child's resistance or spend time explaining the infraction after the time-out ends.	**Do** just enforce the original time-out.
Don't designate a special place or area for time-outs. That just gives the child more ways in which to refuse and cause disruption. Your goal is always to spend as little time and energy on time-outs as possible.	**Do** carry out the consequence exactly where you are when the rule is broken. You can "accuse" the child of completing time-out successfully without having moved an inch. It's the child's perception of the reset that counts in yielding the result.
Don't engage in any discussion or explanation of problems, hold grudges, point fingers, blame or give the consequences in a way that's shaming or humiliating.	**Do** stay in the moment. Keep your cool, no matter what. Be strict, but not stern; use a calm but strong voice. Get the time-out over with and move on to the next moment. Simply deliver the consequence, each and every time a rule is broken, and make a big deal over the child's successful completion of the time-out.
Don't forget to close the time-out; don't give the child control over ending the time-out.	**Do** always notify the child when a time-out has been successfully completed.
Don't allow the child to contribute in any way to whatever's going on while he's in a time-out.	**Do** remember that the child is "out of the game" (of life) however briefly he is in time-out. Keep time-outs short and demonstrate how energy flows readily and generously as soon as the time-out ends.
Don't take a rule breaking as a personal offense ("How could she keep DOING this to me? Is she TRYING to make me mad?") And Don't seek apologies or promises ("Do you promise never to do that again?").	**Do** see the time-out as an interruption of the problem-a diversion, not a punitive consequence. Optimally it serves as a perfect lead in to the next, greater level of new success and a deepening of inner wealth.

Don't try to mediate the child's problem with others.	**Do** watch for broken rules and successes, enforce rules and reflect successes; the rest will take care of itself.
Don't give a time-out in anticipation of a rule about to be broken. If a rule hasn't been broken, you can actually still applaud the success of the choice not to break a rule.	**Do** remember that either a rule has been broken or it hasn't. Expect success. If you expect success, your child will succeed.
Don't back off on the positives when things are going well.	**Do** crank up the positive recognition when good behavior is occurring. If you use positive recognition only to suppress bad behavior, your children will pick up on this, and you'll get more bad behavior. Kids know where the juice is!
Don't turn away and ignore a broken rule. A foot on the line is a foot on the line. Even a tiny bit of a threat or aggression or arguing is still a broken rule.	**Do** maintain a high standard for desired behavior. Never waver when it's enforcement time.
Don't remind children of the rules: "Remember no feet on the furniture. Hey, didn't I just say no feet on the furniture?"	**Do** give time-outs consistently and with no reminders or warnings. If you find yourself repeating a rule, it's time to start enforcing it. If you find yourself thinking, "My children have forgotten the rules," your enforcement needs to be stricter- and you need to make a point of celebrating when that rule is not being broken. Keep commending your children for even the smallest degrees of appropriate effort, attitude and action.

The Ultimate Objective: The Speed Limit Story

The objective is to instill inner wealth, inner strength, godliness, greatness and gloriousness in your children so they awaken to their own internal arsenal and portfolio of greatness and act on it. The reset allows children to realize they won't get what they want along the road they're traveling now. Their actions will only receive attention when they're in the game, playing according to the rules.

Howard Glasser, creator of the Nurtured Heart Approach™, uses a device called the Speed Limit Story to illustrate the need for parents to get out of the way and allow their children to experience the consequences of their actions and decisions. My version of the story goes like this:

I drive fifty miles to work every day. I always take the same route and know that the speed limit on the longest stretch of highway is sixty-five miles per hour. One day I'm not paying attention and find myself going 6sixty-six mph. A police officer stops me with a smile and unceremoniously gives me a ticket for driving too fast. I get the ticket quickly, without any conversation; as he hands it to me the officer tells me to have a nice day and I head to work again. I am not joyous.

The next day I'm really not paying attention and drive eighty mph in the sixty-five mph zone. The same officer pulls me over, unceremoniously and neutrally gives me a ticket without saying a word, hands me the ticket and tells me to have a nice day and off I go to work again. I am really not joyous.

On the third day, I'm running late and praying the officer is nowhere around. I'm doing seventy-two knowing I'm speeding. The officer pulls me over with a smile and unceremoniously and neutrally hands me my ticket. By now, I have learned that the officer is always there, and that he never engages with me as he gives me a ticket. I also know I'm being stopped from getting where I want to go because of my own behavior and I'm taking myself out of the game. I start driving sixty-five on my way to work every day so I can stay in the game and get myself to work on time with a great attitude.

The Light Will Begin to Shine

I believe wholeheartedly that the same kind of light will shine into your child's mind and she'll recognize that she has choices: to break a rule or to obey it. She will gain empowerment with this insight. As soon as she realizes she's in control of her behavior and her destiny, she examines her free will and chooses which behaviors are going to work in her favor. She begins to relax and realizes that she doesn't have to be perfect to gain attention or to be loved. Her mistakes will receive unceremonious time-outs as opposed to harsh, strict, controlling discipline. She soon learns it's far more empowering to make the right choices and stay in the game, because that's where major payoffs live and move and have their being!

So give a consequence when a rule is broken. Do this consistently, day after day. Deliver the consequence in a neutral manner, keep the consequence simple and short, and avoid all forms of warnings, lectures, naggings and angry outbursts. Share lively praise and admiration with your child after the time-out is served and make the "time in" a far better place to be than "time-out." Modify and adjust rules to meet the needs and ages of your children.

Safety First

As a parent, the safety of your children is job one. By all means physically snatch children out of harm's way and refuse to allow them to do things that compromise their physical, emotional, spiritual, and mental safety. If necessary, call the police to help you regain control of a rule-breaking, safety side-stepping teenager, enlist the help of your church or do whatever else is necessary to ensure you are providing adequate protection to your child. But do so with as little energy as possible and get back into the game of success with record-breaking speed as soon as you've regained control of a treacherous situation.

My friend Christine, an expert in teenagers, worked for many years in a group home and had to deal with young boys who were used to essaying angry physical outbursts, foul language and displays of power and control to get what they wanted. One time she ran across a young boy who became very angry when he was told he couldn't go on a field trip. He tore his room apart, piece by piece, and threw every one of his possessions out of a window. Christine sat at the door to make sure he was safe, and ducked as things flew her way. She continued to tell him that she knew he had the ability and power to pull himself together and that she would be there when he was ready to talk and be calm and quiet.

He kept screaming at her, "Why are you not yelling at me?!!"

This young man didn't understand how Christine could remain in control when everyone else he knew would have jumped in to restrain him and tell him loudly how disappointed they were in him.

He finally emptied out his room, slumped onto the floor and began to sob. He eventually composed himself enough to talk to Christine, apologize, and straighten up the room. Christine never again heard a comparable outburst from him.

Another friend of mine had a teenage son who took the family car out for the night. This young man returned the car with a huge dent in the side. Rather than make a scene, my friend calmly asked what had happened. The young boy immediately took responsibility for hitting a pole. My friend shared with his teenager how proud he was that his son would tell him the truth and take responsibility for his actions. Together, father and son outlined a plan to repair the car without any altercation.

Community Service

Older children and adolescents occasionally commit infractions that a time-out will not satisfy. These rules may include not destroying things, not violating curfew, not being aggressive, etc.

If you're using the credit system discussed in the next chapter, an asterisk by a rule denotes that breaking this rule will require community service. Community service should be simple, time-limited and must benefit others (the family, neighborhood, church community, school community, or anyone else you decide on). All privileges and spending go "on hold" until the community service is completed. It's fine for your children to continue earning points for appropriate behaviors; they just can't spend any of it until all community service has been completed.

Community service examples include: emptying the garbage, taking the dog for a walk, raking a neighbor's leaves, cleaning a room of the house, washing the family car, picking up loose trash in the yard, loading the dishwasher, cleaning windows, running errands, etc. Community Service should be based on the age, level of ability and developmental age of the child who receives the assignment. Community service doesn't "punish" your child; it simply offers an additional opportunity for the child to reach more success.

Community service can also be used for children and teens who are not on a credit system. If a major infraction occurs, restrict all privileges until the time-out and community service has been completed.

To make the community service more appealing, when things are calm, seek the assistance of your child or teen while creating it.

Sharing *Parenting Challenging Children with Power, Love and Sound Mind: The Nurtured Heart Approach™ from a Biblical Viewpoint* with your Children and Teens

After you've practiced the recognitions for a while and feel proficient, it's time to enter into the consequence phase. You should also have noticed that since you've begun to nourish your child with recognitions, his inappropriate behaviors are slowly disappearing. This is the perfect time to share with your child what will happen whenever a rule is broken:

1. There will be a short time-out if a rule is broken
2. Parents no longer give warnings, reminders, or second chances
3. Compliance will be mandatory
4. The time-out will start when your child has quieted down
5. The parent will decide when the time-out ends
6. The parent will not speak to the child during a time-out

I know this is hard work at times and will present a few challenges. There will be some tough times and your child will test you in ways you may never have been tested before. So be patient and forgiving with yourself and stand strong. Don't lose heart. You can do this and when you do, you'll enjoy a more peaceful existence even while giving your child additional motivation to follow rules.

What follows will help your child become more responsible, more aware of her feelings and more able to handle them, more capable of handling intense emotions while displaying fewer mood swings, and more aware of the successes and beauty around her. It will help her to recognize and share the greatness and inner wealth she sees in others so she'll make and keep more friends. She will act less impulsively because she can more intelligently consider choices and consequences and handle conflict resolution better. Most importantly, she will begin to realize that she can trust her own internal wisdom and pursue boundless opportunities in life. Because now nothing is impossible — she will see herself as more than a conqueror.

Final Things to Remember

We've spent significant time on rules, limits, structure and boundaries. With all this talk of time-outs, it's vital to the success of the approach that you keep Actively Recognizing, Experientially Recognizing, Proactively Recognizing and Creatively Recognizing your children. Keeping high praise and kudos going when things are going well and making interaction 100% positive and fun will keep your child's portfolio growing in the right direction.

Parenting this Way Can Be Exhausting at First

Whenever I introduce the section on limits and consequences, people get nervous. They say they don't see how it can work or that it feels like they'll be letting their kids get away with bad behavior.

The truth of this new approach is that being relentless and courageous, with clear structure and boundaries, is *more* strict than using occasional punishments that are handed out based on a parent's level of self-control on a given day.

Here's the key: You have to trust the process, trust that God will help you and that He agrees with what you're doing. Have faith, dig in, and discover for yourself just how transforming the new approach really is!

One parent told me that setting limits according to the new approach was "exhausting." That's because every single time you hear, see, smell or taste a broken rule, you must give a reset (time-out). The more consistent you are in this regard, the less you'll witness the same behavior again *providing you're giving them more praise and honor while they're in the game*.

When you and your child are new to the approach, it's true: you'll see LOADS of rules being broken. This is because up till now you've used traditional methods and have corrected without consistency while lending power to negative acts with your own negativity: yelling, scolding, nagging, threatening, etc. It's easy fall into this trap. You'll receive no blame or accusations from me. I mess up at times, too! But if you strictly enforce rules and get your child on the right page, you'll segue from exhaustion to having blessed peace in your home. There will be more time to **enjoy** your children (as opposed to riding herd on them) because they know the rules and will choose to follow them. It will happen at a rapid pace too!

Check Your New Plumbing

We rebuilt an 18th-century farm house from the frame up. When we put in the new plumbing, our plumber took great care to turn on the water for the first time. He waited for the pipes to fill up and then walked around checking for leaks. He did this for a long time because he didn't want to miss a single drip. He wanted to know with one hundred percent certainty that his work was leak proof.

When you begin to use the time-out strategy outlined in preceding pages, you'll want your child to misbehave so you can check for leaks in yourself and allow your child to make mistakes and experience what will happen when a blunder or slip-up occurs. Failure can bring about transformation in and of itself.

The Butterfly Effect

Most of us know the story of how a butterfly is born. A fuzzy caterpillar weaves its own cocoon. While the caterpillar is inside the cocoon, a metamorphosis occurs: the caterpillar becomes a butterfly. When the butterfly is ready to enter the larger world, it pokes at the cocoon and struggles for days to get out of its safe—but terribly confining — space. As the butterfly struggles, it grows stronger until it finally breaks free into the open air and flies away. But realize this: If helping hands come along and rip the cocoon apart to set the butterfly free before its time, the butterfly fails to develop the strength it needs to survive and falls to the ground, dying almost immediately.

We must let our children struggle a bit in order for them to gain strength and wisdom. Keep them safe but allow them to make mistakes, bump into obstacles, dig their way out of dilemmas and experience the challenges and minor hurts of life so they can grow strong and morph into a beautiful creature of God that soars above the heights.

The Lacrosse Game

**Read the story below and come up with as many ways as
you can to implement the strategies and techniques you've
learned to transform the child in it.**

During lacrosse season, a friend asked me to join her at her son's game. I accepted readily, thinking how wonderful it would be to enjoy the outdoors and spend time with a favorite person in my life.

Before the game started, I overheard a young boy, about thirteen, talking to a couple of his friends about their teammates. He was sharing negative feelings he had about them. His friends, more prudent than he, said nothing. Soon they all went away to warm up.

When the game started, the young man became disgruntled with one of the player's actions. He yelled obscenities to the player and stomped off the field at the end of quarter.

The boy's father, the head coach, came over. The two of them got into a screaming match in front of everyone. As they ended the verbal war, the boy threw his cell phone at his father and refused to play. Dad yelled some more about needing his son to play, then walked away to coach the team.

A kind, compassionate father stepped into the fray. He put his arm around the boy and gave him a quick "pep talk." The boy agreed to return to the field but just stood there, unwilling to help his team play during the quarter.

At the whistle, the boy stomped off the field, demanded his cell phone back, and — to my utter shock and surprise — his dutiful dad returned it.

During this break, the boy decided he would re-enter the game as a participating player. When the game began again, he became disgruntled with the coaching skills of his father and gave him a wildly inappropriate hand gesture. Dad did nothing. The game continued with this boy's behavior weaving in and out of acceptable boundaries of respect until the final whistle. The young man, his father and the team celebrated their victory with pizza and ice cream.

This story has stuck with me, even though it happened years ago. I remember standing there, shocked and discouraged.

In a *Parenting with Power, Love and Sound Mind* world, the dad would have unceremoniously reset that young man, then encouraged him for being able to calm himself down and complete the time-out. Dad would then have used positive praise to usher his son back into the game. If the child hadn't agreed to the reset, dad could have walked away and required that everyone steer clear of the young boy until he reset himself. As soon as the child appeared calm, dad could have jumped on that moment as a reset and engaged him with words of encouragement. And about the hurling of the boy's cell phone: there should have been a rule in the family to refrain for twenty-four hours from giving back items that are thrown. Each and every time the young man behaved inappropriately, he should have received a reset, and the reset should have removed him from everyone.

Would it have been tiring for dad to monitor each and every negative behavior? Probably, but the young son is his child. He's responsible to bring this youngster up and move him out of his house as a productive member of society.

I would have recommended to the above dad that he needed to follow the approach as though his son's life depended on it — because it does! This child had many assets and a lot of strengths. He loved the sport, he wanted to win, and he was well-coordinated, physically fit and athletically gifted. He had leadership qualities which, if channeled correctly, could turn him into the next CEO of a major corporation. But these same qualities left unattended could turn him into an angry, bitter soul with a string of jobs because his temper always got the best of him.

In addition to de-energizing the negativity of the boy, it would have been imperative for the coaches to deliciously and descriptively tell the teammates who were behaving and playing appropriately all of the many things they were doing well. This firsthand experience would have shown the one boy how he needed to behave to receive real relationship.

Can you think of other ways you could handle the above situation and stay true to the approach?

Conclusion

When setting consequences and creating limits, consider yourself a referee. You're a neutral keeper of boundaries. You know the rule book cold. Remember, so do your kids! "I forgot" and "I'm sorry, I won't do it again!" doesn't cut it anymore. Enforce the time-out.

Be consistent, clear, structured and tireless as you enforce the rules that govern your household. Be sure the rules are simple, clear and well-defined. Most should start with "No...." (No hitting, no yelling, no running in the house, no driving the dog nuts, etc.). Memorize the mantra that your children already know 99.9% of the rules and any rules they don't know can be taught with Proactive Recognition and time-outs.

Allow children to test the system so they can have firsthand experience with the consequences of their misdeeds and learn for themselves that time-ins are far superior to time-outs. This will create the inner wealth and transformation you want to achieve. Teach your child the approach and remember: always maintain safety above all else.

Questions for Reflection

1. What can you do to help ensure you are acting as a referee when you enforce rules?
2. What are the rules you want to enforce in your home? Write them down in a clear, simple format starting with the word "no."
3. What are some safety issues you must handle as a parent? How can you handle them proactively and how will you manage them without becoming negative or highly emotional?
4. What time-ins can you create that are extra-special to each of your children?
5. What are some community service options you can create for your children?
6. How can you engage your children in the process of creating the rules and enforcing them?

Prayer for Today

Lord, give me the strength, ability and wisdom to powerfully maintain limits, consequences, and structure in my family. Help me provide healthy and helpful time-outs. Teach me new and beneficial ways to create wonder-filled, success-based and fun time-ins that engage and build up my family. Surround my children with angels to provide them with safety. Help me to instruct my children using the time-out mindset and fill them with inner wealth and greatness so they begin to act out who You know them to be. I pray this in the Name of Jesus. Amen.

Chapter 12:
The Credit System:
Training a Child in
Good Stewardship

"The laborer's appetite works for him; his hunger drives him on."
(Proverbs 16:26)

In this chapter I'll introduce you to the Nurtured Heart Approach™ credit system. The credit system is designed to give you a structure and deeper accountability to *Parenting with Power, Love and Sound Mind.* It also gives your child or teen a chance to learn the principles of good stewardship and resource management skills.

The Bible tells us to be wise stewards of the treasures God entrusts to our care and management. The Scriptures mention money and wise stewardship thousands of times and detail what happens when we gather goods wisely, e.g., Joseph, as Pharaoh's money manager, ultimately gathers grain and wealth and saves his family (the progenitors of the nation of Israel and Jesus) from starvation; and what happens when we squander our money and skills, e.g., the Parable of The Talents demonstrates the three workers who are given by their master differing amounts of talents to manage). Unless we painstakingly teach our children from an early age about fiscal responsibility, we can't expect them to behave like anything other than "babes in the woods" when they get out into the world and are invited to take advantage of dozens of credit card offers and other expensive, tantalizing options that will come their way. By imbuing them with an understanding of the price and value of goods, services, and privileges, we give them a firm foundation on which to build a rational approach to spending, saving, tithing and safeguarding their financial futures.

The Credit System is Not Essential for Parental Management

As the ultimate expert on your own family, you alone should decide whether the following credit system will make sense in your situation. But know this going in: in order to make the credit system work, you must dedicate yourself to completing it daily and abiding by its structure. I'm including this chapter solely for those parents who feel you need still another method to help you rear accountable, contributory family members and citizens.

A credit system is especially helpful to parents whose children require extra support and structure. This system helps you remember to energize your child's successes. It influences your child even when she's at school or daycare. It creates compliance with rules and resets (time-outs). And the credit system helps you eliminate warnings and reminders when you interact with your child.

The credit system tunes in to times when your child is experiencing success by not breaking the rules and it isn't adjusted up and down as your child goes through his day. It's not a static system that simply waits (at times interminably in some situations) until your child does something well.

The credit system is another means to instill and enhance inner wealth and greatness. The system's truest function is rooted in the emotional, verbal and psychological affirmations that your child will receive for making positive choices.

The Credit System: A Tool for Creating Success

A highly-organized, detailed and structured method, the credit system helps you create, reinforce and encourage success. It follows the four guidelines of *Parenting with Power, Love and Sound Mind:* providing consistent positive fellowship and presence; celebrating success; de-energizing negativity; and consistent boundaries and limit setting. The approach isn't tiring or arduous. It's custom-made to tap into your child's needs and abilities. By using this method, you create a way forward that floats your child's boat, one that's so appealing she *wants* to participate!

WARNING! RED ALERT! MEMORIZE! The credit system must never be used to discipline or punish. It is a tool to assist you in leading your child into his or her greatness. The credit system shouldn't be used until you've established and consistently used the recognition techniques found in the previous chapters for a reasonable period of time. It's vital that you put into action all of the recognitions first, because the credit system is used in concert with them. Your deep familiarity with the techniques increases the success of the credit system.

My final word of caution is this: the credit system will fail if you don't back it up by honoring your children's successes on a consistent basis. If you decide the credit system is not for you, no harm, and no foul. Just make sure, if you do employ it, that you do all you've learned in the previous chapters and that you "super-reverence" recognitions.

Principles and Benefits of the Credit System

Human Beings Need Resources to Live

Many people haven't a clue about wisely managing available resources. They have trouble giving, saving and spending in ways that bring positive fruit into their financial planning portfolio. Sometimes the failure is complete irresponsibility, but more often it's simply a lack of understanding and training. Everyone who's alive needs sufficient resources to live: food, water, shelter and (in most cases) clothing. None of these are gained without an exchange of some kind taking place. The credit system is a tool to help administer and to teach the need to manage existing resources.

An amazing special education teacher I know created a unique way to teach her students the principles of responsibility, money management and business skills through the use of a credit system.

This teacher makes binders and assigns her students to different positions: bookkeeper, payroll clerk, inventory taker, time clock manager. She prints "money" with her picture and assigns a dollar amount to each bill. The students earn "money" based on the credit system and are immersed in success and recognitions while learning life lessons that will benefit them forever. When her students earn enough "money," they're allowed to buy from her "store," which offers goods and services. The students love the system and thrive under it.

Unlike adults, children and teens have an extremely limited view of how the economy works. I remember when my son, at age six, asked me to take him to the store to buy him a new bike. I let him know I didn't have a new bike in the family budget and couldn't make a major purchase like that. In his matter-of-fact small voice, Chandler informed me that I could simply drive to the bank, put my card in the machine, and money would come out! Even though Chandler knew that his dad and I both worked, he didn't have a clue about the true source or value of the money that so magically emanated from the ATM! A credit system is a tangible, firsthand experience for children and teens to "live" within a resource economy.

The credit system teaches negotiation, bargaining, accounting, spending, saving, and other useful economic matters. The standard chores and allowance system, although easier to manage, is nowhere near as well-rounded or all-encompassing.

Reinforce and Encourage Success through the Credit System

Children and teens with a healthy sense of the economy are far more prepared to succeed in the real world. In stark contrast, people with little understanding of economic realities struggle significantly when they get out into the world. The credit system gives you a chance to transform your child's understanding and relationship to the economy. By implementing a credit system, you constantly provide streams of recognitions as each of your children make positive choices. This keeps everyone moving in the right direction and the greatness of your children occurs as a natural byproduct.

Reinforce and Encourage Appropriate Rule Following, Time-Outs and Behaviors at School and Daycare

A child who needs help behaving appropriately at school or daycare can benefit from the credit system, regardless of the school's policy or opinion on the matter. The credit system method allows parents to give credits to children even when they're away from home. It also shows appreciation for the child in every environment, increasing the child's perception that he's still accountable and responsible while he's away from home. No matter where your child is, there is a sense of empowerment and independence because she knows her choices will directly impact her and her resource system when she gets home to account for her greatness at the end of each day.

How to Design a Credit System

If you've decided to use a credit system, this section guides you step-by-step to craft a system designed uniquely for your child. You'll learn the six necessary steps Howard Glasser developed to implement a successful credit system:

1. Establish the Rules.
2. Formalize a list of positive, desirable behaviors and qualities for which the child can earn bonus credits.
3. Devise a list of chores and responsibilities for which you will award bonus credits.
4. Combine the three lists from above on one large page and title it "Ways to Earn Credits."
5. Devise a list of privileges ("Ways to Spend Credits").
6. Set up a daily review time with your child.

Ten Good Reasons to Use a Credit System

1. It makes boundaries and expectations clear.
2. It keeps the family on track.
3. It promotes consistency and routine.
4. It provides more opportunity for administering emotional nutrition to your child.
5. It is educational; it teaches math skills and critical thinking.
6. It emphasizes finding "what is right with the picture" and creating more moments of success.
7. It can be expanded to include expected behavior while in school, at religious services, at family outings, or any other setting.
8. It encourages the child to take responsibility for positive (and negative) choices.
9. It is predictable and promotes NOT breaking the rules.
10. It is customized to meet the individual needs of each child.

Transforming the Difficult Child Workbook, 2007 (Glasser, Bowdidge and Bravo)

Establish the Rules

1. **Write down the rules so everyone knows and commits to following them.** Clear, concise rules allow your family members to concentrate on their successes and not have to fumble with fuzzy rules or inexact boundaries. Everyone will know the rules and the consequences for not following them. There's power in writing down the rules; it formalizes them so a commitment to them can be made.

2. **Make all rules very clear. Start as many as possible with "no."** No hitting, No talking back, No breaking the rules, No swearing, No shoes in the house, No lying, No stealing, No arguing, No back talk, No disobeying mommy and daddy, No tattling. Create simple, easy-to-follow, understandable rules that make sense to you and your children.

3. **Include only rules that you can monitor and evaluate.** If you don't witness a situation, you can't prove innocence or guilt "beyond the shadow of a doubt." So don't engage in areas where you personally didn't see what happened. Don't allow your children to tell on one another. This creates rivalry and encourages your children to judge and report others. You don't want your child to become the neighborhood or family "police officer." Teach your children to monitor their own behavior, to solve their own dilemmas, and to be responsible. This creates healthy personal power in each of them. Make sure to energize them for the many good decisions and situations they navigate. Encourage them to tell only good things to and about one another.

4. **Include "gimme" rules.** Gimme rules are rules your child might never break or that are easy to do on a regular basis. Put gimme rules in place to help a child earn credits and create success that you can energize with effusive praise and acknowledgment. A "gimme" rule is similar to Creative Recognition. It could be, e.g., go to school every day, wear a seatbelt in the car, wear your helmet when biking, put your pajamas on by yourself.

5. **Establish the number of credits for each honored rule.** Use credit points in any denomination. I recommend that you use multiples of ten. Ten is an easy number for your child and you to remember and tally. If you want to prioritize a rule, simply double its worth.

Formalize a List of Positive, Desirable Behaviors and Qualities for which the Child Can Earn Bonus Credits

1. **Write a List of "Positive Choices/Bonus Credits."** This list will include behaviors, qualities and positive choices you want to encourage and see more often in your child. State the desired behavior or quality in the positive and be sure it's straightforward and easy to understand. Examples: Be polite and respectful, Use good manners, Follow directions, Get dressed by yourself, Share, Help when needed, Be cooperative, Do what you were told even when upset, Complete chores with excellence and without complaint, Stay calm when told "no," Respect the personal space of others, Handle a problem wisely.

2. **Establish the number of credits for each bonus credit you award.** Decide how many bonus credits you'll give for each positive choice your child makes and earns. Keep the points simple to use and easy to calculate. I recommend continuing to use the number 10. If you want to accentuate a certain positive choice, double the number of bonus credits for making that particular choice. If you want to honor an especially good choice, quality or behavior, offer a "Golden Bonus Credit." This is what or when you'll allow your children to spend on a special event or activity because they exceeded expectations in your specified area.

Devise a List of Chores and Responsibilities for Which You Will Award Bonus Credits

1. **Write out the Chores and Responsibilities List.** It's extremely important that this list match your child's age, developmental stage, and ability levels. The younger the child, the simpler the chores and responsibilities.

2. **A "chore" is defined as anything that can be done around the house or neighborhood; a minor duty or task.** Chores can be simple or complex and should make a contribution to the wellbeing of the family. Examples: setting the table, raking the leaves, shoveling the snow, carrying groceries, putting away clothes, folding towels, vacuuming, dusting, mopping, taking out the trash.

3. **A "responsibility" is defined as an activity that is essential to the well-being of the child or the family. It's a behavior that is engaged in on one's own initiative or authority.** Responsibilities are daily facets of life that are crucial to the well-being of the child or family. Responsibilities include brushing teeth, showering, wearing deodorant, completing homework, going to bed on time, eating healthy foods, cooking dinner, watching a younger sibling, feeding a pet, and more.

4. **Establish the number of credits for each chore/responsibility.** This category can vary enormously depending on the level of difficulty, completion time and required effort. Because of this, chores and activities should be assigned points that match appropriate levels of difficulty. For example, completing a research paper may earn 100 points while brushing teeth may only earn 20 points.

Combine the Lists (Rules, Behaviors and Chores and Responsibilities) on one large page entitled, "Ways to Earn Credits"

1. **Combine the Lists on one page.** Make sure "Ways to Earn Credits" are in list form. Write or type them out in a clear, understandable and concise manner.

2. **Earned credits are redeemed to purchase privileges, NOT things.** As you develop your lists, always keep the notion of privileges in mind.

Devise a List of Privileges: "Ways to Spend Credits"

1. **This list should detail the specific privileges you find appropriate for your child, which can be earned through constructive behavior.** Be clear and have all limits in place when you create the privileges list. Privileges must match the age, developmental stage, ability and interest of the child. Some privileges may include going to the movies, taking a trip to the zoo, spending time at the park, one-on-one time with mom or dad, staying up late, maid service, food from a favorite restaurant, sleepover (1 maximum per month), a half-hour of television, radio, or computer time respectively (two hours max per day), gas money, extended curfew, grab bag or treasure chest item, trip to mall, "My Pick" item for dinner, entertainment, chauffeur service, laundry service, etc.

This list is infinite and should match family and child's needs, wai interests and values.

2. **Establish the number of credits each privilege will cost.** Similar chores and responsibilities, privileges can vary. Some privileges more valuable than others and should be "priced" accordingly. ` should also price according to what you want to encourage ` discourage. Place higher prices on things that you want to discour` and lower values on the things you want to encourage. Children over should be earning approximately 200-500 credits per day with a 10 p` system. Children younger than six should be earning on a simpler le at 20-50 stars, tokens or stickers per day.

   All age groups pay for their privileges. Costs and charges are based age, counting ability and developmental level. Individualize according the needs of your children and make it simple so they want to particip` The credit system extends the notion that points and spending need to energetically exciting to your children or the system will fail.

3. **Estimate how many credits your child will typically earn and h much time your child will need daily to use for privileges.** The t` cost of your child's average daily privileges (television, computer, b riding, playing with friends, etc.) should add up to approximately 50 75 percent of the potential total daily credits he or she can earn. T allows your child to pursue their normal daily activities with a bit incentive and effort. It also allows your child to save for bigger, l` frequent privileges, like going to the zoo or getting to do something e that's special. For example, if you create a system where your child ` earn 500 credits per day, 250-375 points should add up to what a ch typically likes to do in a day. This allows the child to save (bank for la use) 125-250 points.

4. **Everything in life is a privilege.** Everything we have in life is a privile` not a right. All humans must pay or trade to get everything they ha` whether goods or services. Keep this in mind as you select privileges ` your list.

5. **Keep "Ways to Earn" list next to the "Ways to Spend" list so both a easy to reference.**

Set Up a Daily Review Time with Your Child

1. **Choose a specific time to review the day with your child.** The daily review is a time to create more relationship and energy for your child. It's a time to convey what went well with the day and to enjoy deeper connection, love and relationship with your child. *It is NOT a time to discuss what went wrong, how things could have been better, or provide a sermon.* The daily review is to continue the *positive* growth of your child's new portfolio. A negative leak here will destroy the rationale behind using a credit system and establish more negativity instead of the positivity you want.

2. **Tally the earned credits and then subtract the privileges that the child purchases.** You can use a notebook, journal, piece of paper, a binder system, chalkboard, whiteboard or a checkbook for the accounting part of this step. This step teaches math and management skills, and allows for a deepening relationship while you track balances. Keeping a written record ensures accuracy and eliminates the need to remember. This is especially important if you have more than one child.

   Take all credits earned, subtract all privileges purchased and bank the rest. You may need to decide when a privilege will be spent. For example, a child who wants to earn points to see a popular movie may reach his goal on a Tuesday night. Because it's a school night, the credits for the movie will be acknowledged and banked for the coming weekend, because the parent decides that's best. When a credit system is implemented, you must be the person awarding the points. This will define you as the person with authority. Award credits based on the rules and regulations of the system. As the child advances, it's fine to let a responsible child take over the system as far as the accounting goes, but you should still maintain the daily review and oversee the accounting to ensure accuracy and offer your undivided attention and energy.

3. **Provide physical markers of success during the daily review.** A marker can be fake money, tokens, chips, homemade markers or anything else you have handy that will work. My favorite marker is different denominations of money with your child's face in place of the president's. This is great for large families because no one can "mix up" the money and the kids love seeing their own picture on the money.

4. Be generous with the credits and give bonus points as they're earned. Reward your child for participating in the daily review appropriately. The goal is to make the child feel successful, loved and wealthy in all areas of his life. This instills inner wealth and catapults her into greatness.

5. Provide some cost-free privileges. Offer family activities that don't cost a thing but increase connection and relationship between you, your child and your family. Cost-free privileges might include reading a book together, watching a movie, playing board games as a family, taking a hike or walking together.

6. During the review, be neutral and objective. Maintain a matter of fact, neutral stance when discussing the daily review. Don't act like a judge, jury, police or inspection officer. This is the time to be a supportive consultant and relay all of the positives that have occurred, the credits earned and the credits spent. When your child sees you in this light, she will also begin to see the world as a safer, easier-to-navigate place. Remember to go from success to success: no lectures, warnings or irritation. On the contrary, when you're reporting the credits your child has earned always acknowledge and show genuine emotion and appreciation for how well he or she is doing. Make a big deal of his successes because that's where he's headed every minute of every day.

Earned Credits are Never Taken Away — They are Only Spent

Credits should never be taken away from a child. If they earned the credits, the credits are theirs to keep. In the event your child doesn't cooperate with you or commits an inappropriate act, credits can be stored or placed on hold (no spending) as a consequence.

Partial Credits are Acceptable, Often Necessary

Partial credit is absolutely acceptable. Partial credit is given under the assumption that it acknowledges behaviors, qualities and positive choices that are beginning to appear with your child. Partial credits are a way to show appreciation for efforts and attempts your children make that are carrying them in the right direction. Partial credit gives your child the insight that you're noticing and paying attention. This gives him even more desire to repeat and enhance the skill until it is mastered. Partial credits work great for improvements in finishing chores and schoolwork or for reducing the number of arguments in the home. Partial credit shows the child that you see and recognize a difference and want to honor the effort she's making.

Using a Credit System for Non-Readers

Customize the credit system to your child's needs and desires. It's fine to use stars, smiley faces, stickers that match the child's interest, or any other symbol that makes the system easier for him or her child to understand. Remember, this is a customized system. Get creative and use whatever you need to establish more success and recognition in a positive light for your child.

Offer "On-the-Spot" and "Spontaneous" Credits

On-the-spot and spontaneous credits are other ways to energize and recognize your child. Award on the spot bonus points to celebrate times when your child does something spectacular and you recognize it by stopping everything and giving bonus points the moment it happens. It's an immediate and unexpected celebration of what has just taken. This type of credit can be for finishing something with excellence or managing intense feelings exceptionally well. On-the-spot credits are great gifts when, for example, a child tells the truth about making a mistake in his favor while adding up points, catches his error, and corrects it. It encourages honesty.

Spontaneous credits can be given when something unusually good happens. A spontaneous bonus is somewhat expected, because you'll place asterisks by items for which you're inclined to give spontaneous points. Example: if your teen consistently breaks curfew, but arrives home on time one day, you might award a spontaneous bonus for it because she acted responsibly. Be sure to make the bonus credits worth earning: 100 or more points. Another good spontaneous credit would be for wise management of the purchasing system. This lets your child know and receive benefits for their fiscal responsibility.

Revise Charges as Needed

As you learn and work the credit system, you may find that you overcharged or undercharged for an item. You may also sense that your child's needs are changing and that modification is necessary. Revision and recalculation are necessary at times and I encourage it. For an intense child, privileges can be altered by making them more expensive. This gives you more influence over his choices and behavior.

Tap into Your Creative Self

When developing the credit system, think about the way your family lives, operates and communicates with one another. Create mock checkbooks for the children to keep track of their credit balances. Email, text or write notes of positive affirmations, encouragement and inspiration along with chores and responsibilities for the day. Hang an erasable board, make a poster board and place it in a noticeable area in the house. Create binders or notebooks. The key is to do something that works for you and your child.

Be creative when you assign points, too. Think Shamu or the Toll Taker. If you want your child to play video games less often and read books instead, assign low points to the books so they're easy to attain and a slightly higher price to the video games. This helps you encourage the behaviors that you want to instill in your child. It establishes new and meaningful ways to invent success and different opportunities for your child to experience.

Include your Child or Teen in the Process of Creating the System

Sometimes a child and teen will amaze you with their creative genius and desires. She can be the perfect partner in creating the system, too, since it will be designed specifically for her. This will give her greater momentum and reason to invest in the process.

Presenting the System to Your Child

Before implementing the credit system, it's imperative that your children (and you!) become familiar with the techniques, strategies, laws and Bible passages that pertain to rewards and work. If so, your child will already be making changes in the way she acts and you'll be feeling a sense of relief. The credit system exists to magnify the successes you current see in your home. Below are some strategies for sharing the credit system with your child.

1. **Present the system in a positive light.** Engage your children by sharing with them how the system will enhance their lives and allow them more recognition and privileges.

2. **Explain the mechanics of the system.** Teach the child every aspect of the system. Explain the Rules list, the Positive Behaviors list, the Chores and Responsibilities list, and the Ways to Earn Credits list. Make sure your child knows how the lists will be managed and which markers will be used. Talk about the daily review session and what it will look like. Be sure your child clearly understands the whole plan to avoid frustration and confusion.

3. **Include your child when developing the system.** Ask for your child's input with regard to the rules, privileges and credits. You can start by showing them some items you have already established or ask for your child to sit with you and do a brainstorming session.

4. **Give "beginner bonuses."** To initiate the system, give a one-time starter bonus in a lump sum. Tell your child the bonus is for their exceptional attitude and behavior in the recent past.

5. **Do NOT take everything out of a child's room or stash all of their possessions.** Doing so will cause a major mutiny. With the credit system, your child learns that things are *privileges* and not *rights*. Keep all the "stuff" where it currently is but remember: if you decide to make television, radio, iPod's, computers, CD's and other customary items a privilege, you'll need to charge for their usage. When you do, your child will have a firsthand experience of the real world's economy.

6. **Charge for privileges that have been enjoyed without permission.** If you see that a privilege has been used without permission or payment, charge the child for it. It's acceptable to let your child know that you may raise the price of privileges he used without permission or payment for that incident.

What to do if a Child Resists the Credit System

In my experience, if a credit system is presented in a positive light, and your children are included in drafting it, most children will be intrigued and agree to comply. If they resist, stay positive and in a neutral manner let them know that the credit system is here to stay. Let them know that all of their privileges are available to them but they will have to buy them with credits to get them. If a major explosion occurs, and your child storms out of the room, stay calm and don't worry. Creating a credit system is a big decision and a major change in structure; something your child may need time to wrap his mind around. Give him private time to think things through and process his feelings. When he comes back, more than likely, he will agree to participate. When he does, make sure you value his choice, share appreciation and recognize that this was a big decision.

If a child still doesn't want to use the credit system, you'll just have to "wait out" the resistance. Take deep breaths, stay calm and neutral. Occasionally let the child know he will have credits available to purchase something as soon as he's ready. Continue providing recognitions and accruing credits for your child and banking them. Your goal is to remain immovable and pull the child into success. Don't threaten, nag, yell or punish them. Do continue to verbally reward your child with delicious doses of energy with every success you see. Just hold your ground and keep the energy level high. The resistance is temporary.

How Long Does it Take to See Improvement and Benefits?

Credit system benefits begin within the first two to eight weeks. It takes four to six weeks to create a new habit, so keep that in mind as you're learning and negotiating the new system. Your children will begin to feel an internal sense of responsibility and will learn to enjoy the structure. For children who have used negativity to meet their needs, a shift toward positivity slowly occurs and parents who were viewed as "evil," "critical," and "mean" now become "supportive" and "wonderful." The child begins to view parents as the people who let him or her know in great detail how exceptionally well they do on a day-to-day basis.

Do I Need to Stay on the Credit System for Life?

As the last word in your house, only you can decide when it's time to go off the credit system. Never leave the decision up to your child. Review the reasons you decided to go on the system in the first place. If your goals were met and the system seems to have lost its reason for being, it's probably time to move on. I do recommend that if you implemented it, at least complete two months of the credit system so everyone can walk away with new skills and successes. If you start and stop it within weeks, it will have lacked "staying power" and teachable moments.

Expect to be Tested

We've already discussed that it is a child's job to test the limits, structure and boundaries that a parent puts into place. This is how they learn to live in and view the world. When your child tests you, remain strong, neutral, and argument-, worry- and negativity-free. Simply state that the only way to have privileges is to earn them. Continue to super-energize successes and give consequences for rules that are broken. Your positivity and relentless pursuit of success will allow you to pass the test.

Chapter Summary

Children will continue to make mistakes no matter which parenting techniques you use. But when you use *Parenting with Power, Love and Sound Mind,* your children will become accustomed to moving from success to success and will naturally desire to do the right thing. When they do make a poor choice, they typically will recover from it on their own, quickly and effectively. They take responsibility for their actions and live with increasing amounts of integrity.

In this chapter we've reviewed an optional credit system for parents to use with their children, how to teach the system to children, and what to do if they refuse to participate.

The credit system has emotional and educational benefits. Keep the system simple and flexible and only stop using it when your goals have been reached. Be sure to follow the intention of moving your child from success to success with the system.

Questions for Reflection

1. What are the pros and cons of developing a credit system in your family?
2. How can you tap into your artistic self and create a system that will build up your children and allow them to flourish?
3. Will you include your children in the creation of the system? Why or why not?
4. Design a credit system that reflects your family's needs and values.

Prayer

Lord, help me to see if a credit system will benefit my family. If a credit system is the path You want, please guide me so I can create one that is beneficial to my family, fun to follow, and becomes a solid learning experience. Thank You that You are a God that supplies exceedingly, abundantly above all that we ask and think. Thank You for wanting my child to know how to use and manage life resources ably. Thank You for giving me the gift of the credit system and using it as a tool to provide more skills for my child that allow my child to flourish and follow Your vision for his/her life. Help me use the credit system to give my child the skill of being an exceptional manager of resources. Allow this system to teach my child how to give, save and spend. Thank You for making my child spiritually, emotionally, physically and financially prosperous all the days of his/her life. I pray this in the glorious Name of Jesus Christ. Amen.

TRANSFORMING SCHOOL AND BEYOND

In this section we will discuss how to take *Parenting Challenging Children with Power, Love and Sound Mind: The Nurtured Heart Approach™ from a Biblical Viewpoint* to school. You will be asked to creatively come up with ways to engage all the people with whom your children and teens interact with so they receive nurturing from every area and facet of their lives.

Chapter 13:
Taking the Approach
to School and Beyond

"Train-up a child in the way he should go and he will not depart
from it." (Proverbs 22:6)

In this chapter we'll discuss how to extend the transformation you're experiencing at home to your child or teenager's school. Not all children who have issues at home will have issues at school, so this chapter may not apply to you and you can skip ahead to the conclusion. But if you're the parent of a child who also has issues of a similar nature while in school, this chapter will help you find ways to foster success at a distance and keep everything on track. Please also note that you can use ideas from this chapter to help you outside of the school setting. For example, use your creativity to take the ideas of this chapter and use them with your child's coaches, church youth groups and day or after-school care.

The beginning of Proverbs is devoted to the teaching of Biblical wisdom and how important it is to attain and achieve. Biblical wisdom brings great success to one's life. The acquiring of Biblical wisdom is most desirable and necessary to experience long life, the blessings of Abraham and all the promises of the Bible. To be students of the Bible it is helpful to know history, some math (if you want to know money, weight, height, length, size), reading and language. This means you will need a little knowledge of those subjects or have someone knowledgeable available to you. To that end, it's imperative to ensure that your child or teen is getting a solid education and learning things that will benefit him in life. Taking the approach to school and beyond will help increase your child or teen's performance and success when outside of the home and in academic, athletic or church activities.

Today's Teachers Marinate in Pressure

I've worked with many school teachers in a variety of settings and can confidently confirm that today's teachers have horrendously difficult jobs.

Teachers are under immense pressure to adhere to their curriculum and to make sure their students reach desired levels of achievement on standardized tests. Most teachers work with limited resources and a sense of isolation from other adults. All are required to multi-task.

Adding insult to injury, the needs and intensity levels of children and teens are increasing today. Most teachers aren't equipped to adequately meet the needs of intense students: riding herd on the compliant ones is daunting enough, considering everything else that's on a teacher's plate!

One teacher told me that although she is a Masters level teacher, she has never been offered a course in classroom management. She said she has been trained to teach, but has no clue how to manage the emotional and social issues that arise on a daily basis. Most teachers' usual methods work well enough for the average child but not for the marginal or intense child.

Teachers learn the same problematic traditional methods that parents learn about dealing with children. Teachers use warnings, lectures, yelling and other negativity-laden means to settle down an intense child. Those who don't, usually try to gently quiet the child. Neither of these options work because energy and relationship are transmitted at the wrong times. The misbehaving child is no better off and the teacher remains at square one having "rewarded" the child for inappropriate conduct. To compound the matter, classroom limits and consequences may be so fuzzy that constant testing of boundaries becomes the best game in town, with predictable results.

A good friend recently earned a teaching certificate at a nearby university. She finished her student teaching in an inner city elementary school and graduated with a Masters in Education. On graduation day, she told me she would never set foot in a schoolroom to teach again. For her, the stress of working with predominantly intense children was overwhelming. A woman who dreamed for years of being a teacher and educating young children, imparting wisdom and knowledge to them, started the profession for all the right reasons and ended up leaving over something completely avoidable. Teachers need new skills in their tool boxes!

Please remember all this as you talk with your child's teacher about your decision to carry *Parenting with Power, Love and Sound Mind* into the classroom with regard to your child. Proceed gently, respectfully and with compassion as you ask for the help of your child's teacher. I commend all parents who are willing to bring the approach to school for their children.

If a teacher is open and wants to learn, he'll not only help you create additional success for your child, but he'll learn how to do it for an entire classroom of livewires. The more the approach is spread, the more children, teachers and other caregivers will reap the benefits of transformation, peace and success. So there's plenty of benefit in it for all concerned; it just takes a little time, and a teacher's willingness, to improve.

Introducing the Approach to Teachers

No matter how you choose to connect with your child's teacher — by direct contact, e-mail, phone, or letters — be sure you remain positive. Share the benefits you've already achieved at home and provide a ready-made checklist (you'll learn more about this later in the chapter), and eagerly welcome any questions and feedback.

I feel strongly that direct contact is the best way to introduce the approach. In a face-to-face meeting, let the teacher see how genuinely pleased you are with the accomplishments and successes that your child has achieved at home. It's also helpful to bring a copy of this book, *Transforming the Difficult Child Workbook (Glasser, Bowdidge and Bravo)* or *The Inner Wealth Initiative (Glasser, Block and Grove)* for the teacher as a gift. This gives the teacher the opportunity to learn more on his or her own time and not feel additional pressure from you to make a decision on the spot. By spending time with a book on the subject, the teacher should realize the transformative power of the approach and consider adopting it in the classroom.

If the teacher isn't quite ready to adopt the entire approach for his or her classroom but is willing to work with you, you can use the checklist approach and see if, over time, the teacher begins to see the benefit to and the improvement in your child. If you follow a credit system, the nightly review of the checklist will spotlight the rewards your child should receive according to his or her behavior at school. If you don't follow the credit system, you can still use a checklist for school but you'll have to "super-honor" your child for all the good choices he made during the day. The purpose of this is two-fold; the child becomes aware that what he does while away from home is important to you and he realizes he's accountable to you for his behavior even when you're not with him. Also it gives him more opportunities for success and to be energized in more significant ways.

If your child attends public school, the teacher may or may not be willing to learn to educate from (*Parenting with Power, Love and Sound Mind*) they may flat-out refuse to try. Your next stop might be the principal of the school; the last resort would be the district office. Going directly to the district office first would probably incite the principal; he or she would feel blindsided. Go up the steps of the hierarchy and see if you can gain support at a higher level.

Persistence may be necessary, but it must be gentle, positive persistence. All public school children, regardless of any formal diagnosis, who have behaviors that interfere with their own learning or the learning of others, are entitled to reasonable accommodations. Asking a teacher to fill out a short checklist is a reasonable accommodation and takes less than a minute of time.

If your child attends a private school, your visits should be first, to the teacher, second to the principal and then on to the pastor or Board to which they are accountable. Again, persistence is necessary, but proceed gently until the chain of command or the teacher warms up to the idea of giving the approach a trial run.

Using the Approach with Elementary Age Children

1. **Create the checklist.** The checklist is a simple, easy to follow, easy to complete piece of paper or index card. It's easy to read and understand for both the student and teacher. On it, the teacher will have all the information she needs to assess your child in class. The teacher should only need seconds to fill it out. It's best if the teacher has input in creating the checklist to be used because she may notice things that happen in school that don't happen at home.

2. **Some sample rules and positive behaviors for the checklist:** Paying attention, completing class work on time, no name-calling, sitting quietly during reading time, staying in seat, raising hand to ask a question, no bad words, following directions, no talking when others are talking, eating lunch neatly, using good cooperation, being kind and considerate,

sharing appropriately, writing neatly, staying focused on tasks, class participation, playground behavior, no touching others, etc..

3. **Meet with the teacher or send a note or e-mail.** Remember the rules: Stay positive; keep the meeting brief; share the essentials of the approach and how dramatically they have improved your child's behavior at home. Explain how using the checklist and the approach will make the teacher's life easier and won't require much effort on the teacher's part. Verbalize the good qualities you see in the teacher. Let the teacher know that you want to extend your child's new success to school. This collaboration will make the teacher's job a little more stress-free and it will increase and promote good behavior in your child. Share the checklist with the teacher and make multiple copies so he or she can just pull one from a folder. Make sure the teacher understands that the approach is designed to increase the positive skills, talents, abilities and character qualities within your child and to give your child stronger coping skills, a sense of power over his feelings, stronger decision-making skills and a greater sense of responsibility. The child should exhibit better behavior as a result of being held accountable for his actions; a great selling point to teachers. Mention that the approach is easy to implement and learn and that it works great in homes and schools all over the country and internationally.

4. **Decide the frequency of contact you want with the teacher.** You'll need to let the teacher know whether you want daily or weekly contact and what days you want the checklist sent home with your child. It's best to specify daily contact or at least that every Friday the checklist be brought home by the student.

5. **Your child is responsible for bringing the checklist home to you.** If you're on a daily schedule, your child can give you the checklist when she gets home from school, during the daily review time, or during homework time when the backpack is out. If you're using a credit system, you can award points for every successful checklist she hands in to you.

6. **Explain the checklist to your child.** Explain to your child that he'll have more opportunities to show off his success and earn credits toward his credit system while he's attending school. Show him the system and explain how it works. Ask for his input and ideas about the list. The more

SCHOOL BEHAVIOR SUCCESS CHART

Student Name _____   Date _____

REWARD WORKING FOR: _____

POINTS: 2 (mostly)   1 (sometimes)   0 (rarely)

	Student Rating before lunch	Student Rating after lunch	Teacher Rating & Initials
Followed Rules			
Stayed on Task			
Completed Class Assignments			
Turned in Homework			
Displayed Appropriate Friendship Skills			
Other			
DAILY TOTAL POINTS EARNED			

Comments _____

_____

_____

invested in the list he is, the more success he'll attain. Be sure your child understands that he will be accountable at home for rules that are broken at school even if the school already provided a consequence. Tell your child he's responsible for ensuring that the list gets home to you whenever it's supposed to come home. If the list doesn't make it home, credits will not be earned and a time-out will be given.

7. **Refueling your child.** Your child has been away from you all day and seeks relationship with you when she sees you again. It's important to give your child positive energy when she re-enters your presence after a significant absence. If she's used to getting her needs met in a negative way, is stressed out or has had a bad day, she may try to engage you in an inappropriate way (crying, pouting, looking sad, looking angry). If this happens, say something kind, maybe give a hug or a pat on the back, and energize her for any positive behavior you see.

8. **If your child receives a poor rating:** Let your child know what will happen at home if they receive a poor rating at school. If he knows this in advance, he'll understand on a deeper level that he will be held responsible for his choices and behavior. You should give a pre-established, energy neutral time-out in your home. Keep the time-out short, and don't get pulled into negativity; instead, energize only any success you see. Follow the same plan if you need to assign community service. Set your intention on moving from success to success and treat the indiscretion as if it means nothing to you.

Using the Approach with Middle School and High School Children

1. **Create the checklist.** The concept will be the same as for the younger children, but the checklist will probably have four to six teachers on it unless you deem it necessary to concentrate only on certain classes. **See the examples below to aid you in the creation of a checklist.**

2. **Sample rules and positive behaviors for the checklist:** Paying attention, completing class work on time, no name calling, sitting quietly during lecture, staying in seat, raising hand to ask a question, not using bad words, following directions, no talking when others are talking, cooperation with lab partners, being kind and considerate, sharing appropriately, writing neatly, staying focused on tasks, good class

participation, appropriate dress, no excessive public displays of affection, no touching others, homework completed, entering class on time, coming to class prepared, etc..

3. **Meet with the teachers.** Most schools will be able to accommodate a meeting with all of the teachers through the guidance counselor's office or the special education department. The principal can also facilitate a meeting. If schedules don't allow for you to meet with the teachers, work with the guidance counselor or social worker in the building. Follow the rules above: be brief, be positive, explain the benefits of the approach and how it has helped your child, explain the need to move it to the school and that the checklist and the approach will create a better teacher-student experience between your child and staff. Tell the staff how the checklist will be handled at home (with good and poor ratings). Come prepared to give every teacher and person in attendance a copy of the checklist with a letter of explanation. Advise the teachers that *your child,* and *not a teacher,* is responsible for making sure the list gets to each teacher, gets signed and gets brought home. Make sure the teacher understands that the approach is designed to increase the positive skills, talents, abilities and character qualities within your child and to give your child stronger coping skills, a sense of power over his feelings, stronger decision-making skills and a greater sense of responsibility. Mention that the approach is easy to implement and learn and that it works great in homes and schools all over the country and internationally.

4. **Decide the frequency of contact you want from the teachers.** You will need to let the teacher(s) know if you want daily or weekly contact and which days you want to have the checklist sent home with your child. I recommend weekly.

5. **Your child is responsible to bring the checklist home to you.** If you're on a daily schedule your child can give you the checklist when he arrives home from school, during the daily review time, or during homework time when the backpack is out. If you're using a credit system, you can award points for every successful checklist he hands in to you.

6. **Explain the system to your older child or teen.** Explain to your child that she will have more opportunities to show off her success and earn

HIGH SCHOOL BEHAVIOR SUCCESS SYSTEM

Student Name _____ Date _____

Inner Strength/Greatness	English	Math	Social Studies	Science	Elective(s)
Competence					
Demonstrating Leadership					
Following Directions					
Good Attitude					
Participating					
Completing Assignments					
Use of proper language					
Responsible					
Good Cooperation					
On time and prepared					

Comments _____

_____

_____

Teachers: Please assign a number to each Inner Strength and Greatness Competency as follows: 0 Poor; 2 Fair; 3 Good; 4 Very Good; 5 Excellent:

credits toward her credit system while she's in school. Show her the system and explain how it works. Ask for her input and ideas. The more invested in the list she, the more success she'll attain. Make sure she understands she will be accountable at home for rules broken at school even if the school already provided a consequence. Tell her she's the responsible person for getting the list home to you on the specified days. Let her know that if the list doesn't make it home, credits won't be earned and/or a time-out will be given.

7. **Refueling your older child or teen.** All children, even older ones, need to be refueled and energized by you when they see you again after a significant absence. Don't fall into negativity or get trapped in lectures, nagging, warnings or sermons. Stick to the plan of super-praising success and providing no relationship for negativity. Give recognitions for bringing the checklist home, getting it completed, and for all successes and award points if you're using a credit system.

8. **If your child receives a poor rating:** Let your child know what will happen at home if she gets a poor rating while at school. If the child knows this in advance, she'll understand on a deeper level that she's being held responsible for her choices and behavior. You should give a pre-established, energy neutral time-out in your home when she gets a poor rating. Keep the time-out short, don't get pulled into negativity, and congratulate all successes. Follow the same plan if you need to assign community service. Set your intention on moving from success to success and treat the indiscretion as though it means nothing to you.

Added Benefits of Taking the Approach to School

There are many benefits to adding the approach to your child's school regimen. The child will be known by the teacher on a more intimate and powerful level. This increases accountability at school. Academic skill level tends to go up when a child feels he is valued and cared for by a teacher. If your child and teacher were at odds with one another earlier, the new approach reduces the tension as the teacher experiences the emotional and social growth of your child.

In addition to better adult relationships, your child will experience more social success. The approach helps intense children manage and navigate issues that once challenged them. This makes them more likeable and acceptable to other children. The majority of children whose parents use the approach begin to nurture others shortly after learning what's going on. The happier the child is at school, the more he'll want to be there.

At school, the approach also gives your child a sense of accountability to you. Even though you're not at school, your child knows she must bring home a checklist of her day. This increases her motivation so she experiences increased verbal recognition at home and at school. It also increases relationship between you and your child. Think about it. If you ask your child how school went, he typically says "fine" and moves on. The checklist allows for deeper, more meaningful conversation to take place and for you to get a true sense of what your child's day looked like.

Chapter Summary

In this chapter we discussed the reasons to use the approach in school and the benefits of extending the approach to classrooms. We provided guidelines for speaking to and working with your child's teacher and sample checklists for you to consider. The goal of extending the approach to school is to give your child additional opportunities to achieve success and to learn to experience the approach outside of the home. The approach creates a better teacher-student relationship, increases your child's likability and friendships, and allows for deeper relationship with you.

Questions for Reflection

1. Do you believe it's necessary for the success of your child to have them follow the approach at school?
2. What do you think is the best method of communication between the teacher and yourself?
3. In which major areas do you want to receive feedback and information?
4. Create a success sheet and a way to encourage your child's teacher to partner with you.

Prayer

Father in heaven, help me to implement this approach in my child's school. Open the minds and hearts of the staff and administrators to hear about this approach and adopt it into their school system. Lord, help this extension of the approach create more skills, friendships and responsibility in my child. Thank You for making my child academically, athletically and socially gifted. Help them to excel at all they touch at school, at church, in all of their groups, activities and sporting events and to be able to stand up for what they believe is right. I pray this in the Name of Jesus, Amen.

VICTORY

In this final section we will review what
you have accomplished to date.
You will be encouraged to live victoriously by
allowing the Biblical principles and the
techniques of the Nurtured Heart Approach™
to infiltrate the way you interact with all of the
people in your life. May you prosper in all
areas of your life. Ignite and fan the fires
of greatness wherever you go!

Conclusion

"To Achieve Your Dreams Remember Your ABC's. Avoid negative sources, people, places, things and habits. Believe in yourself. Consider things from every angle. Don't give up and don't give in. Enjoy life today: yesterday is gone, tomorrow may never come. Family and friends are hidden treasures, seek them and enjoy their riches. Give more than you planned to.

Hang on to your dreams. Ignore those who try to discourage you. Just do it. Keep trying, no matter how hard it seems — it will get easier. Love yourself first and most. Make it happen. Never lie, cheat or steal, always strike a fair deal. Open your eyes and see things as they really are. Practice makes perfect. Quitters never win and winners never quit. Read, study and learn about everything important in your life.

Stop procrastinating. Take control of your own destiny. Understand yourself in order to better understand others. Visualize it. Want it more than anything. 'Excellerate' your efforts. You are unique of all God's creations, nothing can replace YOU. Zero in on your target and go for it!"
(Wanda Hope Carter)

A Standing Ovation Just for You

Please, take a bow and receive the standing ovation of applause and cheers now being sent your way. If you walked through this book, slowly and strategically putting the teachings into action, you're now well on your way to transformation. You should be noticing your calmer, gentler and happier child. So take some credit for what you're seeing; you deserve it. You've just completed a book that, when put into action, will change your life forever. If you devoured this book in one sitting because it fascinated you and you needed all of the information before putting into action, I challenge you to start now. You are a parent that engages your children with power, love and sound mind.

I would like to take a moment and review the wonderfully beneficial journey we've just completed. We started by discussing what your new home could look like and asking you to come up with a miracle vision for your family. Moving on we learned that we're fighting for the success, safety and well-being of our children. Afterward, we realized that God is the only perfect parent. It is acceptable for us to make mistakes because we simply dust off, forgive ourselves and start again. We are the best we can be at this point in time. The importance of Guarding Your Heart, Mind and Words came next, followed by Developing Positive Portfolios: The Law of Reaping and Sowing.

When the foundational sections were completed, we moved to the Transforming Communication and Interaction section where we learned all of the recognitions: Active Recognition: Unconditional Acceptance; Experiential Recognition: Character and Value Education; Proactive Recognition: Rules for Life and Creative Recognition: Making Requests that Get Results. The recognitions are vital to the success of the model and should be used as often as possible.

The next sections we covered were the all important Transforming Limit Setting, Consequences and Structure chapters. Here we learned that true discipline is used to teach and train your child and teen and to actively set and impose limits and consequences. We finished up this area by taking the approach in totality and creating a credit system to help you and your child stay on track.

The final section was about taking the approach to school and beyond. We learned what to do to transport all the benefits of the program to an academic or other setting to ensure accountability even when your children are away from home.

Now, It's Your Turn to be filled with Power, Love and Sound Mind

You've learned all of these marvelous tools and mindsets to help you with your child. Now it's time to reflect a bit on the condition of your own life. It is my hope that as you read through the chapters you realized that all these wonderful blessings are not just for your child. We have worked hard throughout this book to gain greater parenting skills, but in this chapter, I want to help you find your own inner peace. God wants you to live life full-out and to fulfill all of your passions and purposes in this lifetime. If you're already doing this, hats off to you. If you're not walking in a manner you want and experiencing total fulfillment, it's time to put the principles to work for yourself, too!

Just because you live in a bigger body than your child and have more worldly experience, bumps and bruises, doesn't mean that God has placed a "Stop Work" order on your dreams and goals. He wants you to live to your potential and know your own inner wealth, inner strength, godliness, gloriousness and greatness. If you're thinking you can't be used by God, know this: God has always used the ordinary and the outcast to serve him. Read the Bible if you have any doubt about that! Simply start where you are and with what you have — and watch how He'll grow you!

What is stopping you?

"My deepest fear is not that I am inadequate. My deepest fear is that I am powerful beyond measure. It is my light, not my darkness, that most frightens me. I ask myself, 'Who am I to be brilliant, gorgeous, talented, fabulous?' Actually, who am I not to be? I am a child of God. My playing small does not serve the world. There is nothing enlightened about shrinking so that other people won't feel insecure around me. I am meant to shine, as children do. I was born to make manifest the glory of God that is within me. It's not just in me; it's in everyone. And as I let my light shine, I unconsciously give other people permission to do the same. As I am liberated from my own fear, my presence automatically liberates others." (Marianne Williamson)

Is fear keeping you from allowing yourself to be all you can and want to be? In most cases, the voice of fear is false and misleading. A helpful acronym for inappropriate fear is this: False Evidence Appearing Real (F.E.A.R.). Its core strategy is to keep you in bondage to it, to prevent you from becoming all you can be. Fear comes in many forms. Here are some of them:

Fear of what people might think or say about you or your family. Fear can cause you to hide your light and life lessons from others. It can also keep you from challenging yourself to squarely face and conquer whatever it is in your circumstance that keeps you from the success that God has placed before you to win.

Fear that whispers, "You're not good enough, strong enough, attractive enough, smart enough..." The list is endless — and simply false!

Fear that tells you, "You don't deserve anything or anyone good, special, nice or important in your life." As a child of God, you deserve every good thing that His kingdom offers, including peace that passes all understanding and release from the bondage of F.E.A.R.

Fear of the future and what it holds. The Bible assures us: *"For I know the plans I have for you,' saith the Lord. "Plans to prosper you and not to harm you; plans to give you hope and a future." (Jeremiah 29:11NKJV)*

Fear of lack — lack of resources, talents, skills, time and energy. Each of us has 24 hours, each and every day, to pursue goals. Have others done what you want to do? They have the same number of hours you do, not a millisecond more. Does F.E.A.R. ever try to convince you that you'll never have enough of whatever it takes to allow God to bless you?

Fear of change. Change is inevitable. Getting from first to second base takes changing from foot to foot and from breath to breath. "A journey of a thousand miles begins with a single step." Often taking just a few small steps is all that's required of you to align yourself with your God-given potential to succeed.

Fear of dreaming too big. As Marianne Williamson so brilliantly reminds us, "playing small does not serve the earth." If you aim for the stars and miss, you don't fail. Instead, you'll likely find a beautiful cloud to call home, or you'll learn how to adjust your aim so that the next time you try, you'll reach a star!

Fears are so prevalent in human beings that hundreds of clinical names have been devised to describe them, from Achluphobia (fear of darkness) to Zoophobia (fear of animals).

As you look at your life and at what you want, fear has the potential to blind and paralyze you, keeping you from achieving your God-given potential. But this is what God says:

"For God has not given us a spirit of fear and timidity, but of power, love, and self-discipline." (2 Timothy 1:7)

Conquering your fear is not easy, but it's worth it! Conquering fear is where real blessings begin. Victory against fear doesn't come overnight. It takes time and small, incremental steps to reach the place you want to be. Start your battle against fear by doing one small thing that you would normally have avoided or said "no" to out of fear. By doing this, you embark on a journey that will change your life and allow you to realize your God-given purpose with a clear vision.

Start Sharing your Inner Wealth and Greatness with Yourself Now

Whether it's fear, frustration, worry, a perfection-oriented mind, a sense of lack, not measuring up or whatever else is holding you back from knowing yourself and your purpose, it needs to stop now. Adopt a vision for your life that matches your values, interests and desires. Live with intention and clean up your thoughts and words to match the new you, the "You" that has always been there but has been kept under wraps. Now is the time to get moving with fierce determination toward your goals. If you're not sure where you're supposed to go, ask God and He will make your path clear.

Everyday, throughout the day, actively and experientially recognize and super-boost, invigorate and pump yourself up. Follow these simple examples to get you started.

"I am a glorious human being filled with honor, integrity, courage, and dignity. I speak the truth in love and work hard to provide for my family. I am uniquely created by God to do good works."

"I am special to my family. I contribute many skills, talents and abilities to the well-being of my family, my church and my community."

"I am powerful, responsible and an inspiration to others. My clear mind is filled with wisdom, knowledge and understanding. I seek to share what I know with my family and others to edify and help them. I am caring, cooperative and a great example to my children."

One Marine's Story

My husband, Brian, has a good friend who is in the Marines. This friend, whom I will call Sergeant Jones, is someone who knows how to live with a heart-filled intention and vision, and has done so ever since he was a child. Sergeant Jones grew up taking care of three siblings and a crack-addicted mother. He had no father or male role model. Sergeant Jones told my husband that he knew from a very young age that he didn't want the life he was given. He refused to accept that he would be addicted to drugs like most of his family; gang-bound, impoverished, unemployed and uneducated.

Many people told him he would go nowhere and would amount to nothing. He continually discounted this information and told himself he was better than his environment. He considered himself a person of worth and value, with strengths and gifts, a person who deserved to have all that the American dream has to offer.

Sergeant Jones put himself through high school and enlisted in the Marines. The Marines gave Sergeant Jones a family unit and stability. He is happily married with grown, successful children and remains highly-esteemed in the Marines. Sergeant Jones took his circumstances and created new ones with the power of his mind, words and actions, and is now completely content with the life he has led.

Practical Ways to Make the Approach a Top Priority in Your Life

To keep the approach as a top priority as a parent and as an individual, be attentive in your attitude and behavior. Katherine Teasdale Edwards tells in her seminars that athletes training for an event can't take more than one or two days off during training. If they take off three days in a row, they'll be back at the beginning of their training physically.

Following the strategies and structure of *Parenting with Power, Love and Sound Mind* will take consistency, diligence and effort. Maintaining focus is essential in creating the miracle you want to see in your home.

**Tips for taking care of yourself so your inner wealth
and greatness can shine**

1. Pray, praise and worship, meditate, keep a journal.

2. Get proper rest.

3. Eat healthy foods.

4. Drink plenty of water.

5. Say "No" to tasks, committees, projects that do not fit into your schedule.

6. Ask for help when you need it.

7. Get organized, de-clutter and simply your life.

8. Allow extra time to do things and to get to places.

*9. Plan and schedule tasks, changes and projects over time.
    don't procrastination.*

10. Live within your means.

11. Enjoy the moment and take one day at a time.

12. Laugh.

13. Surround yourself with people you love and admire.

14. Forgive.

15. Talk less and listen more.

16. Slow down.

17. Be grateful for all that you have in the moment.

Some suggestions to stay engaged:

1. Pray daily that God will keep you moving steadfastly to follow the Nurtured Heart Approach and life philosophy of *Parenting with Power, Love and Sound Mind.*

2. Keep a copy of this book by your bedside to review for a few minutes every night. Evening refreshers keep you motivated and ready to start anew every day.

3. Keep a journal, noting changes that you see in your child and family. Reflecting back from beginning to end helps you to see how far you've come and the positive results you're now experiencing as a result of remaining diligent with the approach.

4. Start a support group for parents. Support groups are beneficial because you'll be able to receive insights from other parents, you'll be accountable to others, and you'll be more willing to make efforts to follow the approach.

5. Continuously check back to the website (nurturinglifeconcepts.com) for regular announcements that let you know when "check-ups" will be available, or to contact Wendy via e-mail, telephone or "snail" mail to schedule an appointment, consultation, training or seminar.

A Success Story:
Daniel and Cathy's Story

Daniel and Cathy are dedicated Christians who regularly attend and volunteer their time at their local church. They're wonderful people who have four children. Their eldest son is an adult who lives on his own. Alexander and Cassidy, ages 12 and 9, respectively and a newborn infant, still live in the house. The family was referred to me by an assistant pastor because they needed some help with Alexander's behavior at school.

When Daniel and Cathy arrived, we began to chat and I knew right away they were people who would embrace *Parenting with Power, Love and Sound Mind*. It was so apparent they loved their children and would do whatever was best for them. As I taught them the basic principles of the approach, they soaked it in like sponges. I recommended they should come back in three weeks to a full day of training I was offering and they jumped at the opportunity.

Flash forward to the full-day training. Daniel and Cathy came and brought a guest with them who was equally excited to learn the approach. Daniel and Cathy were ignited with inner wealth and greatness. Cathy was so delighted to share the transformation she had seen in her children in just a few short weeks that it almost looked like I planted her in the audience and paid her to be in the training!

Daniel and Cathy advised the other trainees that the approach had created a renovation revolution in their family. By simply noticing times when things were going well and descriptively providing strengths-based language, their children's behavior became exceptional. The couple created velocity in their home, moving their young ones from success to success. The children were sharing, playing together, fighting less and basking in the glow of their newly-tapped strengths. Daniel and Cathy were reveling in their own success and in the ease of the approach. They felt in more control, relaxed and proud of themselves.

Cathy, a preschool teacher, was so impressed with the results of the approach that she began using it on the children in her class. To her amazement, the approach worked there, too! She noted that the customarily well-behaved children who were not getting nurtured and filled with positivity were asking her to include them by saying something nice about them, too!! Cathy began sharing the qualities and characteristics of good leadership, concentration, team work and cooperation with her students and they began living up to that expectation.

At home Cathy would use combinations of Active Recognitions, Experiential Recognitions and Proactive Recognitions with Andrew and Cassidy. She would say things like:

"Alexander and Cassidy, I see the two of you watching television and sitting quietly. This shows me that the two of you are in control, able to relax and enjoy time together without fighting. These are qualities of greatness in the two of you that I am so proud of."

"Alexander, you were able to go to school today although school is hard for you. Andrew, you stayed the whole day, completed your work on time, shared and talked politely with friends and followed the rules of the classroom. You are a person of power and self control. You are responsible and strong on the inside."

"Cassidy, you cleaned your room without fussing or fighting. This tells me you respect me and our house. Caring for your possessions and living with good hygiene shows that you are a person who desires the best for herself and is thoughtful."

Daniel and Cathy also shared the simplicity and beauty of "resetting" their children. Initially, they didn't think it was going to work. They had to make some adjustments to accommodate the needs of their children. For example, the reset works best for Cassidy if she's given a designated place to go, but Alexander can reset anywhere. At first the children tested mom and dad, but in a short time they began responding.

Cathy and I ran into each other a few months after the seminar. She was still delighted and doing well with the approach. She even commented how the pastor's message of the day fit right into the approach philosophy. His message was about forgiveness for self and others when a mistake or sin is committed and moving with "terminator type" determination into the next moment of success.

Cathy and Daniel swapped problem-oriented language for solutions and strengths-based language and turned their household around quickly. Cathy is vivacious, fun, positive and filled with love and God-given vision for herself and her family. She is a woman of greatness and inner wealth."

Daniel is calm, cooperative and insightful. He's a gentle and kind man who cares deeply for his family and loves providing for them as a man of God. I'm confident that the two of them will continue the approach with confidence and victory!

You should be seeing these changes in your children following *Parenting with Power, Love and Sound Mind:*

• Believing that God sees them as great, unique, worthy of love and attention, filled with skills, talents and abilities that are useful to this world and to God himself.
• A world view that is positive and hopeful.
• Better relationships with all of the people in your life.
• A more balanced, God-centered way of living.

The Most Important Commandment is Love

"The most important one (commandment) answered Jesus, is this: Hear, O Israel, the Lord our God, the Lord is one. Love the Lord your God with all your heart and with all your soul and with all your mind and with all your strength. The second is this: Love your neighbor as yourself. There is no commandment greater than these."
(Mark 12:29-31)

As our journey comes to a close, remember that *Parenting with Power Love and Sound Mind: The Nurtured Heart Approach™ from a Biblical Viewpoint* is based on this commandment. Walk in love, grace, mercy and forgiveness with everyone you encounter, especially with your most valuable gift from God-your children and teens.

"That the communication of thy faith may become effectual by the acknowledging of every good thing which is in you in Christ Jesus."
(Philemon 1:6)

As you walk in love for God and for others you also need to speak and think highly but humbly of yourself. In his marvelous book, *Sparkling Gems from the Greek,* Rick Renner shares that the word "effectual" in the verse above is the Greek word "energeo" from which the word "energy" derives its origin. This word effectual or energeo literally means to activate or energize yourself and the things that God has placed in you. We do this by studying the Word of God, being confident in our knowledge of Christ and who we are in Him. This confidence allows us to confess with our mouths the victory we have and the success we see in others. (*Sparkling Gems from the Greek, page 713; Rick Renner (2003)).*

Another Round of Applause!!

Wow! You have completed this book and learned so many new things, put them to use and have begun to see the fruits of your labor. Thank you for allowing me the honor of being part of your new plan. I hope you see that you are instrumental in allowing your child's God-given godliness, gloriousness, greatness to shine through. You have empowered your child and everyone around you to live life as world changers. Because you took the time to be a light and a leader in your family, you've given them the most generous inheritance of all: inner wealth and greatness. I appreciate your deep understanding that your children need more than traditional methods to reflect the greatness that is in them. Your innate ability to recognize that your job is to raise your child to be a God-loving productive adult has allowed you to parent in the "now" with an eye carefully placed on the future. I'm grateful for your courage and strength to forge into this new territory with zest and perseverance. Thank you for taking your responsibility as a parent seriously and holding great intentions for your children. Please continue to remain teachable, love deeply and nurture everyone you meet.

Points and Questions for Reflection

1. Name some creative ways you can ensure continuation of the approach, principles and philosophies in this book?
2. What is the current condition of your portfolio?
3. Write down all of the positive strengths, talents and abilities you see in yourself and share them with someone close. Ask that person to add more of your assets, ones you didn't see yourself. Look at the list often.
4. Train yourself to use the recognitions on yourself and other adults and on other children in your life as often as possible throughout your day.

Prayer

Lord, thank You for helping me and giving me all the tools I need to be a parent who is *Parenting with Power, Love and Sound Mind.* Give me the ability and perseverance to stay dedicated and focused to succeed with the approach. Carry me and my family into Your vision for us and give us the ability to fulfill our entire God-given dreams, passions, purposes and intentions. Place people in my life that follow the approach and have similar mindsets so I have support from others. I am so blessed to be a child of God and to have You in my life. I submit to You and love You. In Jesus Name I pray. Amen.

How long does it take to see results with *Parenting Challenging Children with Power, Love and Sound Mind: The Nurtured Heart Approach*™ *from a Biblical Viewpoint*?

Teachers and parents have reported immediate results with *Parenting with Power, Love and Sound Mind*. If you fearlessly and relentlessly pursue the techniques of the approach you will see dramatic results very quickly. Full implementation of the model should occur within one month.

Where is the Nurtured Heart Approach™ being used?

The Nurtured Heart Approach™ is currently being implemented all over the world as a parenting model. Many people use this approach in their homes and report dramatic improvements in all of their relationships as well as a greater sense of peace and joy in their lives. The Nurtured Heart Approach™ is used as a social curriculum in hundreds of U.S. and international schools and has been proven to increase teacher retention and reduce the need for medication, Individual Education Plans, suspensions, referrals, excessive absences and other disciplinary methods.

Do kids get addicted to (or prideful from) constant positive feedback?

No. Authentic, heartfelt feedback given to children or teens helps internalize accomplishments as their own. They will change negative behavior based on appropriate positive feedback. When the behaviors and successes are internalized as something they "own," children and teens no longer work out of a negative portfolio. They recognize their worth and strengths and act out of this new set of beliefs.

What is the best strategy for implementing the approach in a divorced family?

It's ideal when both parents are on the same page with any parenting approach. But if this isn't an option, one parent can engage unilaterally with your child or teen, helping to instill inner wealth and good judgment so that your child can cope with stress and adapt to changing environments more readily. Parent your child with power, love and sound mind and God will sustain all the work that you are doing even when the child or teen is not in your immediate presence.

My child is on medication and I would like to take him off. How should I go about doing this?

I commend you for wanting to take your child off medication. However, that is a decision that should be made with consultation and assistance from your doctor. If you cannot find a doctor who will help you take your child off medication please go to the following website www.ICSPP.org. They may be able to assist you in locating someone who will help.

Why should I praise my child for doing what is expected?

Children and teens need help to learn their value. By creating success for them and showing them that they have worth and purpose, you are helping them to grow into the person God designed them to be. As a parent, educator, caregiver or therapist, your primary job is to acknowledge and honor what's "very good" about every person you meet and help. By accentuating the skills, talents and abilities you see in a child or teen you are helping them to grow into the person God designed them to be; to see the light of God in each person and what you believe they can be.

Can *Parenting Challenging Children with Power, Love and Sound Mind: The Nurtured Heart Approach*™ *from a Biblical Viewpoint* be used at home and at school?

Absolutely! Children and teens that have issues and challenges at home usually have similar issues at school. We have yet to meet a teacher who has refused to use the Nurtured Heart Approach™ with students. Its ease and simplicity allows for dramatic changes at school, which makes quick believers out of teachers! In the event you do have a teacher unwilling to try our approach, we can show you how to use the system exclusively at home. And don't worry: the results will soon "spill over" to create success at school.

Why is this approach so useful with challenging children and teens?

When children live in an environment that treats them as "outsiders" or "adversaries," they form negative impressions of the world and of themselves. And this impression is punctuated every time they receive relationship and connection through adversity. Traditional parenting methods often confuse the situation and exacerbate it because the child or teen mistranslates the punishment *as a reward.*

The goal of *Parenting with Power, Love and Sound Mind* is to let the child or teen know that there is no genuine relationship in negative or adversarial behavior; that real relationship can only be planted in "good soil" (positive behavior). Positive behavior builds trust; negative behavior destroys it.

In a series of well-designed steps, success is created by actively and accurately acknowledging progress and by laying down a foundation of easy-to-understand limits and boundaries. When the challenging teen realizes that the only way to gain relationship is to follow the rules with trustworthy, positive behavior, he or she stops mistranslating the word "relationship" and begins the quest to locate and honor his or her inner wealth and everyone else's!

Can I use *Parenting Challenging Children with Power, Love and Sound Mind: The Nurtured Heart Approach™ from a Biblical Viewpoint* with all my children, even if some do not have behavioral issues?

Yes. *Parenting with Power, Love and Sound Mind* should be implemented with all of the children and teens in your family from the very beginning. It's perfectly acceptable to provide more intense intervention with your most challenging children, but the approach should be used across the board with all of your children and teens.

What if my child or teen is so challenging that I can't find anything nice to say?

We have worked with parents who have felt this way — and said so. If you're in the same boat, listing to one side and paddling with a broken paddle to the best of your weary ability, but not making any more progress, take heart. No doubt you feel isolated, misunderstood and upset with everything you've tried to this point. *Parenting Challenging Children with Power, Love and Sound Mind: The Nurtured Heart Approach™ from a Biblical Viewpoint* will help you and your child or teen to **create** success, proactively and creatively recognize each success, and block access to the arteries and capillaries that feed the negative relationship. ***By following these steps you can have the relationship you have always wanted with your child.***

Will this approach work for single parents?

Yes! *Parenting with Power, Love and Sound Mind* is easy to implement and takes very little time to do. Five minutes a day can change the entire dynamic in a house. Single parents can find great success with this approach. Implement the approach and watch, amazed, as your child or teen becomes more team-spirited, cooperative and kind. You'll be completely in control of yourself and aware of your relational output when it comes to parenting your children and teens. Just as you will believe in your child or teen's greatness, you will learn to see that greatness in yourself. It's a fact- You can't see the amazing qualities in others if you don't already have them in yourself!

Can I use this approach with my special needs children and teens?

Parenting Challenging Children with Power, Love and Sound Mind: The Nurtured Heart Approach™ from a Biblical Viewpoint is an excellent choice for children with Attention Deficit Hyperactivity Disorder, Oppositional Defiant Disorder, Pervasive Developmental Disorder, Autism Spectrum Disorders, Bi-Polar Disorder, Anxiety, Depression, Phobias, Emotional Disturbance and many other disorders and challenges.

It has also been successful working with children who display any of the following behaviors or characteristics: temper tantrums, bed-wetting, alcohol and drug abuse, sexual promiscuity, poor social skills, disrespect, strong-willed, low self-esteem, sibling rivalry, poor impulse control, inability to focus, anger and defiance issues, authority challengers, feelings of being misunderstood and stubborn, struggling in school, truancy, loners, and many other challenging issues.

How does this approach match up with Scripture?

Jesus Christ was the ultimate teacher, nurturer and model of perfection. In His ministry forgiveness was readily available to even the worst offenders. The "reset, restore and recover model" used in *Parenting Challenging Children with Power, Love and Sound Mind: The Nurtured Heart Approach™ from a Biblical Viewpoint* opens the door to forgiveness so you and your child or teen can get back into the enjoyment of life.

Jesus rarely yelled, screamed, nagged and physically forced people to change their ways. He taught people when they were engaged and listening to him. *Parenting with Power, Love and Sound Mind* will teach you how to share the lessons you want your children to learn when they are emotionally available and when you are able to communicate at your best level.

The Bible is the Christian's life source and guide. It provides us with structure, rules and advice on how to live and breathe in every situation. *Parenting with Power, Love and Sound Mind* will teach you how to provide clear and consistent limits, rules and structure within your family so that it functions at a higher, predictable level.

Jesus also taught us who we are in Him and what we have access to because we believe in Him. We are the head and not the tail, we have power, love and sound mind, wisdom, utterance, discernment and the list goes on. Using *Parenting with Power, Love and Sound Mind* will teach you how to instill the inner wealth, inner strength and godliness, gloriousness and greatness of Jesus in your children and teens.

Parenting with Power, Love and Sound Mind should never be considered as a replacement for the Bible or the work of Jesus Christ in our lives. The approach resonates so clearly with our Christian Value system that we can adopt and use it almost instantaneously without compromising our core beings.

Where do I go to learn if my child or teen is just behaving age appropriately?

That is a very good question. Well-meaning caregivers often think something is wrong when their child or teen is actually behaving according to plan. Please go to www.nurturinglifeconcepts.com to download your free copy of Child Development.

This guide will review ages and stages·from birth to eighteen years of age. It will assess their expected physical, emotional, social, mental and moral development as well as other areas of interest.

What are some practical ways to build inner wealth and inner strength in my teens other than using communication and interaction?

Build inner wealth and inner strength into your child or teen by getting them out of the house and involved with the world around them. Choose activities that your child or teen will enjoy. If they are old enough, encourage them to volunteer in the community, at church or in their school. Check into local Parks and Recreations programs, YMCA, dance classes, acting and theatre lessons, horseback riding, summer camps, Boy and Girl Scouts, ski clubs, gymnastics programs, school clubs, Mommy and Me programs, reading programs, art classes, Karate, Tae Kwon Do, church youth programs, golf lessons, bowling leagues, baseball, cheerleading, basketball, soccer, swimming lessons, music lessons, football, cooking instruction, learn a foreign language classes and many more activities.

How can I Increase my child's social and friendship skills?

I talk to many distraught parents who wish their children and teens had more friends. *Parenting with Power, Love and Sound Mind* implementation alone will enhance social skills and a sense of belonging in your child or teen. When they begin to internalize that they are valued, loved and needed, children and teens typically begin to take healthy social risks and interact on a more comfortable level with peers. In addition to using the model with your children and teens, here are just a few quick practical tips to help you increase their chances of building friendships. Teach them: proper eye contact, conversational skills (questions, comments, and interests to share when talking to friends), personal space (remain arms length distance from others), and sharing. Role play different friendship-making skills with your child (make up a scenario your child is likely to encounter and act it out with them). Most importantly, instruct your children in the principles and strategies of *Parenting with Power, Love and Sound Mind* so they can use the skills with others.

What does a *Parenting Challenging Children with Power, Love and Sound Mind: The Nurtured Heart Approach*™ *from a Biblical Viewpoint* play date look like?

Invite children with similar interests over for brief periods of time. Stay close by. This is time to build their skills and inner wealth, NOT "me time." Actively nurture and strengthen all positive play and interaction. Plan fun activities: board games, video games, movies, the park, playground, zoo, museum, a restaurant, swimming, trip to the library, create a craft, make treats, bubbles, sidewalk chalk, backyard tag, etc. Only point out the positives using lots of liveliness!

I have really implemented *Parenting with Power, Love and Sound Mind* with my family. What other practical tips do you suggest that can increase success in my family?

Bring on the Food! Feed your family a diet filled with protein (lean meats, fish, beans, nuts and seeds), milk, fresh fruits and vegetables and whole grains. Have a drink! Give children and teens plenty of water throughout the day to maintain optimal hydration. Get up and out! Encourage children and teens to be physically active at least one hour per day. Rest! Ensure your children are getting the recommended amount of sleep for their age and ability. Children and teens may need between 8-12 hours of sleep for maximum health. Give up the junk food! Reduce and limit soda, candy, sweets, treats and foods high in saturated fats. Seek the advice of your family physician for a plan that best fits your family's overall health and wellbeing.

How do I help my anxious child or teen with *Parenting with Power, Love and Sound Mind?*

Put worry, misery and doubt behind: Provide super lively, descriptive and engaging communication and interaction during times when things are going well! Teach proactively and creatively- Never while your child or teen is anxious. When they're anxious, simply let them know that you know they have the personal power and skills to get through their situation. Teach helpful breathing: Breathe deeply in through the nose and exhale deeply through the mouth. Count to ten. Visualize a place of comfort: beach, mountain, stream, playground, flying in the air like a superhero above it all, etc... Instruct on physical relaxation techniques: Have your child or teen slowly tense one body part at a time and release and relax each part until the whole body is relaxed. Coach your child to visualize or actually "throw away" their worries in the trash. "Cast their cares."

How do I manage the most difficult times of the day- the morning routine, meal times, homework, bed time, chore time and transition times?

These high stress danger times can become fun and productive with *Parenting with Power, Love and Sound Mind.* Simply trusting and following the steps in this book will create change in the way these times are experienced. First create structure and organization so the children and teens are not surprised. Help children and teens manage time. Share all that is going well before, during and after the moment. Be sure you are powerfully acknowledging and recognizing strengths and skills throughout the day: Be proactive and creative.

APPENDIX A: PRAYERS TO PRAY OVER YOUR CHILDREN

The Power of the Blessing and Declaration

"....whatever you bind on earth will be bound in heaven, and
whatever you loose on earth will be loosed in heaven."
(Matthew 16:19)

Realize that the condition of your heart, thoughts and words is vital to the mental health and well-being of your children. Speak words of appreciation and genuine truth when you see behavior that is awe-inspiring and grand, and declare over your children what you want to manifest. Practice setting intention and vision. Lay your hands on your child, as the Spirit moves you, and declare over them a word of hope, health and wellbeing, promoting empowerment and prosperity in their lives.

In my experience, children love to have words declared over them by the people of authority in their lives. They hear it, soak it in and embrace it. Here are a couple examples of blessings found in scripture:

"May God himself, the God of peace, sanctify you through and
through. May your whole spirit, soul and body be kept blameless at
the coming of our Lord Jesus Christ." (1 Thessalonians 5:23)

The Priestly Blessing: "And the Lord spoke to Moses saying: Speak to
Aaron and his sons, saying, This is the way you shall bless the
children of Israel. Say to them: The Lord bless you and keep you; the
Lord make His face shine upon you, and be gracious to you; The
Lord lift up His countenance upon you, and give you peace. So they
shall put my name on the children of Israel, and I will bless them."
(Numbers 6:22-27 NKJV)

If you're new to sharing blessings over your child, the above verses are good places to start. In the appendix, I've also added blessings derived from Scripture which are wonderful to use. When you feel confident in your ability to declare blessings, I encourage you to create your own special blessings, derived from Scripture. A sound blessing will convey your child's uniqueness, skills, talents and abilities. It will also demonstrate a clear picture of their destiny. Finally, it will be a declaration for their safety and favor.

A blessing that my husband Brian and I regularly pray over our children follows. With hands gently placed on a child's head, shoulders or back, we say with genuineness and in faith: "I declare this child belongs to the Lord. This child is a leader and not a follower, the head and not the tail, is blessed coming and going, is blessed in the city and the country; this child is obedient to me and to You and will experience prosperity and long life. This child is filled with peace, patience, kindness and gentleness in all instances. Because this child walks in faith and divine love, he/she will experience freedom and favor with all people. Angels, encamp this child and protect him/her in all of his/her doings. This child is highly favored by God and man; because he/she walks in the way of the Lord, he/she will be abundantly blessed in all he/she does. I declare this in the name of Jesus. Amen."

Proclaim a blessing over your children daily, before they leave home and at bedtime. It will help you impress on their hearts who they are in Christ.

(As you read aloud the Scriptures below please insert your child's name. Continually feast on the Bible and find Scriptures other than these that touch your heart and speak directly to the need you are having with your child.)

"And we know in all things God works for the good of (my child) who loves you and has been called according to your purpose. God foreknew (my child) he also predestined (my child) to be conformed to the likeness of his Son, that he might be the firstborn among many brothers. He predestined (my child) and called (my child), he also justified (my child) and he also glorified (my child).

"No temptation has seized (my child) except what is common to man. And God is faithful; he will not let (my child) be tempted beyond what (my child) can bear. But when (my child) is tempted, he will also provide a way out so that (my child) can stand up under it." (1 Corinthians 10:13)

"....But (my child) will be filled with the fruit of the Spirit which is love, joy, peace, patience, kindness, goodness, faithfulness, gentleness and self-control." (Galatians 5:16, 22-23)

"I have not stopped giving thanks for (my child) remembering (my child) in my prayers. I keep asking that the God of our Lord Jesus Christ, the glorious Father, may give (my child) the spirit of wisdom and revelation, so that (my child) may know him better. I also pray

that the eyes of (my child's) heart may be enlightened in order that (my child) may know the hope to which he has called (my child), the riches of his glorious inheritance, in the saints, and his incomparably great power for (my child) who believes. That power is like the working of his mighty strength, which he exerted in Christ when he raised him from the dead and seated him at the right hand in the heavenly realms, far above all rule and authority, power and dominion, and every title that can be given, not only in the present age but also in the one to come. And God placed all things under his feet and appointed him to be head over everything for the church, which is his body, the fullness of him who fills everything in every way." (Ephesians 1:15-23)

"I pray that out of his glorious riches he may strengthen (my child) with power through his Spirit in (my child's) inner most being, so that Christ may dwell in (my child's) heart through faith. And I pray that (my child), being rooted and established in love, may have power together with all the saints, to grasp how wide and long and high and deep is the love of Christ, and to know this love that surpasses knowledge-that (my child) may be filled to the measure of all the fullness of God." (Ephesians 3:15-19)

"I am confident that he who began a good work in (my child) will carry it on to completion until the day of Jesus Christ. And this is my prayer: that (my child's) love may abound more and more in knowledge and depth of insight, so that (my child) may be able to discern what is best and may be pure and blameless until the day of Christ, filled with the fruit of righteousness that comes through Jesus Christ-to the glory and praise of God." (Philippians 1:6, 9-11)

Psalm 23, Psalm 91, 1 Corinthians 13:1-13, Colossians 1:9-14 and Ephesians 1:3-8 are also good confessions to bless your children and teens.

APPENDIX B:
HELPFUL WORDS
TO USE WITH
YOUR CHILDREN

A joy
A good friend
A hard worker
A source of strength
A leader
A light
A lighthouse
A helper
A scientist
A great example
Advocate
Aware
Accomplishing a lot
Acting creatively
Acting spirited
Admirable
Appreciative
Attentive
Attentive to detail
Being dazzling
Being inspiring
Being powerful
Being wise
Brave
Bringing out the best
   in others
Beaming
Choosing what's
   important
Compassionate
Considerate
Cooperative
Creative
Courageous
Constructive
Clear
Clear minded
Committed
Courteous
Dedicated to success
Diligent
Discerning
Direct
Dignified
Deeply understanding
Demonstrating integrity

Exceeding Expectations
Easy to like
Efficient
Empathetic
Expansive
Feeling the joy of
   discovery
Flashing a contagious
   smile
Finding new in the
   ordinary
Faithful
Focused
Forgiving
Generous
Going above and beyond
Gracious
Genuine
Good hearted
Glorious
Having unique qualities
Having great curiosity
Handling strong
   emotions well
Having an open mind
Honorable
Hopeful
Independent
Inspiring
Inquisitive
Intelligent
Possessing innate ability
Just and Fair
Kind
Loving
Looking out for others
Managing time well
Making a hard task look
   easy
Making great choices
Making an insightful
   inference
Making delightful
   deductions
Making a solid educated
   guess

Organized
Open minded
Pulling together
Patient
Positive
Peaceable
Peaceful
Powerfully spirited
Productive
Passionate
Reasonable
Respectful
Respecting Self
Refined
Responsible
Seeing the big picture
Self-controlled
Sunshine to others
Steadfast
Strong on the inside
Trustworthy
Thankful
Thrifty
Tactful
Thoughtful
Understanding
Using a pleasant voice
Using your great mind
Vibrant
Visionary
A quick mind
Brilliant thoughts
A pleasant manner
A fine sense of humor
A wonderful sense of
   beauty
A great appreciation
   of art
A great sense of logic
A great ability to
   be receptive
Amazing forethought
Balanced thinking
Excellent planning skills
Good team work
Imagination

Knowledge of when
   to reflect
Magnificent thinking
Perseverance
Real talent
Zest
Beauty
Being present
Connections
Devoted
Enthusiastic
Grace-filled
Displaying gratitude
Hospitable
Imagination
Joyful
Desiring Justice
Listening
Searching for meaning
Nurturing
Openness
Playful
Questing
Reverent
Good use of silence
Teachable spirit
Transformational
Creating unity
Wonder-filled
Yearning for more.....
Zeal
Embracing differences
Having gusto
Cherishing moments
Cherishing opportunities
Altruistic
Amazed/Amazement
Ambitious
Amiable
Attractive
Calm
Carefree
Careful
Certain
Cheerful
Comfortable

Comforting
Competent
Composed
Concerned for others
Confident
Congenial
Coordinated
Creative
Delighted
Delightful
Desiring the best for
   others
Determined
Driven toward a goal
Easy going
Encouraging
A desire for excellence
Excited
Fabulous
Fascinated
Fantastic
Friendly
Gentle
Glad
Good natured
Happy
Healthy
Helpful
Neutral
Nice
Obedient to safe
   authority
Optimistic
Outgoing
Patriotic
Persistent in reaching
   vision
Pleasant
Polite
Powerful
Rational
Reassuring to others
Relaxed
Resilient
Rested
Good sense of safety

Sensible decision maker
Sentimental
Serene
Sophisticated
Special
Strong
Motivated
Successful
Supportive
Sure
Sweet
Terrific
Truthful
Uninhibited
Warm hearted
Making others feel
   wanted
Willing to try
Wise
Wonderful
Worthwhile
Knowledgeable

Author Biography
Wendy A. West Pidkaminy

Wendy is a Licensed Clinical Social Worker, Certified School Social Worker, Adjunct Professor, Advanced Trainer in the Nurtured Heart Approach™ and the Director of Nurturing Life Concepts, LLC.

Wendy has diverse and vast experience in the public and private sector. She has worked with numerous non-profit organizations, churches, for-profit companies, government agencies, school districts, universities and colleges as well as in private practice bringing transformation, vision and healing to countless individuals and families.

Wendy is an engaging, dynamic speaker who regularly travels sharing God's Word, strengths-based, solution-focused principles, *Parenting Challenging Children with Power, Love and Sound Mind: The Nurtured Heart Approach™ from a Biblical Viewpoint* and a vast array of other topics in trainings, retreats, consultation, curriculum building and seminars.

She lives in Upstate New York with her husband, Brian, and their two children, Savannah and Chandler. They have two dogs; an English Bull Dog, Daisy and Chocolate Lab, Molly.

If you are interested in contacting Wendy for counseling, life or parent coaching, sharing a testimony or to book her for a speaking engagement please go to:

www.nurturinglifeconcepts.com,

send her an email at:

wendy@nurturinglifeconcepts.com

or mail her at:

131 West Seneca Street Suite 139, Manlius, New York 13104.

Editor-in-Chief Biography

Kristine M Smith lives in Washington State. She is the author of five books. Kris's collaboration with Wendy Pidkaminy began in 2008 when Wendy tapped her to edit and enhance three e-books she was writing. The collaboration continues, to the immense joy and satisfaction of both women. You can reach Kris at kristinemsmith@msn.com, see her copywriting portfolio at http://kristinemsmith.elance.com, and follow her blog at http://almostfamousbydesfault.blogspot.com.

Additional Products by Wendy A. West Pidkaminy
Available at www.nurturinglifeconcepts.com

Jimmy and Julia's Rainforest Adventure: Discovering Healthy Power, Love and Sound Mind (2009). Written by Wendy A. West Pidkaminy and Illustrated by Rhonda K. West. This book is a whimsical children's book that teaches youngsters the value of using Howard Glasser's Nurtured Heart Approach™.

All Day Workshop: Training Teachers How to Implement the Nurtured Heart Approach™ in the Classroom (2009). Facilitated by Wendy A. West Pidkaminy and Co-facilitated by Advanced Trainer and Kindergarten Teacher Andy Palumbo. DVD and Audio CD.

Parenting Today's Children with Power, Love and Sound Mind (2008). Wendy A.West Pidkaminy, Free E-book.

Your Life Purpose and Vision: 5 Common Roadblocks on the Way to a Successful Future (2008). Wendy A. West Pidkaminy, Free E-Book.

Finding Real Healing with Non-Traditional Christian Counseling (2008). Wendy A. West Pidkaminy, Free E-Book.

Additional Books by Howard Glasser, M.A.

Transforming the Difficult Child: The Nurtured Heart Approach™ (1999) by Howard Glasser and Jennifer Easley.

101 Reasons to Avoid Ritalin Like the Plague AND One Great Reason Why It's Almost ALWAYS Unnecessary (2005) by Howard Glasser and Melissa Lynn Block.

The Inner Wealth Initiative-The Nurtured Heart Approach™ for Educators (2007) by Howard Glasser and Tom Grove with Melissa Lynn Block.

Transforming the Difficult Child Workbook: An Interactive Guide to the Nurtured Heart Approach™ (2008) by Howard Glasser, Joann Bowdidge and Lisa Bravo.